"This is a truly elegant book from a truly elegant bar. Maison Premiere has always followed a path of its own—sophisticated, historically informed, but never stuffy—and *The Maison Premiere Almanac* does the same. It's restrained, focused, and more than a little amusing, all things I wish I saw more of in modern drink books—or indeed books in general."

—DAVID WONDRICH, editor-in-chief of *The Oxford Companion to Spirits & Cocktails*

"Elegance, excellence, and quirky celebration have been the defining characteristics of the magical Maison Premiere in Williamsburg since the bar opened. I'm excited to see these qualities beautifully captured in their new book that highlights oysters, absinthe, and more."

—DANA COWIN, founder of *Speaking Broadly* and former longtime editor-in-chief of *Food & Wine*

"I'll never forget the first time (or the second and third time, for that matter) I visited Maison Premiere. I thought to myself, "This place is so original, so beautifully imagined, so thoughtfully designed, and just so damned good." No one is at Maison Premiere by accident, and everyone (including the winning team) seems to be so pleased with themselves for choosing to spend a portion or all of their evening there. Had I ever heard of Sazerac or absinthe before my first visit? Of course. Had I ever had a better version of either? Never."

—DANNY MEYER, founder of the Union Square Hospitality Group

"Maison Premiere's ability to reach for the magic in all things has always been what makes it great, and their almanac is drunk with that same spirit. I will visit this book when I am homesick for another moment in time, and whenever the current one calls for something truly extraordinary."

—JORDANA ROTHMAN, food writer and cookbook author

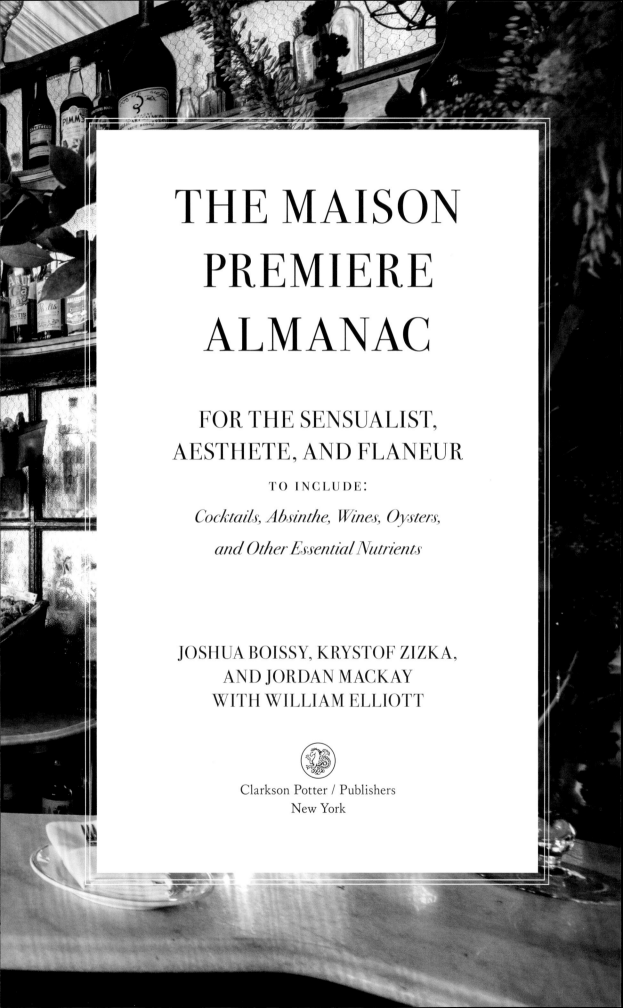

THE MAISON PREMIERE ALMANAC

FOR THE SENSUALIST, AESTHETE, AND FLANEUR

TO INCLUDE:

Cocktails, Absinthe, Wines, Oysters,

and Other Essential Nutrients

JOSHUA BOISSY, KRYSTOF ZIZKA,
AND JORDAN MACKAY
WITH WILLIAM ELLIOTT

Clarkson Potter / Publishers
New York

CONTENTS

PREFACE 9

1. THE PLACE 13

Modest beginnings; historical and geographical inspiration; appearances and design; artisanal collaborators; bar people; gardens

2. THE BAR & ITS DRINKS 41

A dossier of refined tools and advanced techniques; a lexicon of Maison Premiere spirit selections and outlooks; tableside preparations; a brief note on a beer and a wine; the glory of Muscadet; and an omnibus of cocktails, classical and original

3. ABSINTHE: THE SONG OF THE GREEN FAIRIE 179

The tumultuous, sometimes tawdry history of an ethereal spirit; how we found absinthe and why we chose it; thoughts on drinking it; proper absinthe service and cocktails

4. THE CALL OF THE SEA 213

The mighty oyster; oyster-bar inspirations; discovery of old New York's oyster obsession; clams and other oceanic animals; oyster-ordering empowerment, salubriousness of oyster eating

5. THE ALMANAC. 245

A calendar of events; oyster wines; more sea delicacies; poetry and song; New Orleans streets; precious artifacts; horticulture

ACKNOWLEDGMENTS 264

INDEX 266

PREFACE

on the almanac form; how to corral a vexingly diverse subject into a book; and the rare combination of style and substance

I WAS FIRST BROUGHT TO MAISON PREMIERE BY A FRIEND WHO knew I would like the place. At the time, which was a few years after Maison opened, I lived in San Francisco but came often to New York. As I drank an excellent cocktail, marveled at the intricate layers of interior design, perused a shockingly canny wine list (especially for a place recognized as a cocktail bar), and swallowed supremely pristine oysters, I thought to myself, "Where did this place come from?"

Making it even more mysterious was the absence of any authorial signature. While a well-dressed gentleman stood at the door to lead us to our table, he was not the owner. Nor, it turned out, was anyone in the room. No one seemingly cared to take credit for this impressive act of creation.

It would be a few years later that I would find myself sitting down at a table over seafood and drinks with Joshua and Krystof, the men responsible for Maison Premiere, talking about the possibility of adapting their precious vision into book form. We parted company that night not with a concept but with the knowledge that we liked one another and the promise of working together.

The concept would take a while to hash out. After all, given the realities of selling a book these days, Maison's inability to smoothly fit into any category posed a problem. Like the old cities that inspired it—New Orleans, New York, and Paris—Maison is a haphazard collection of diverse influences, whose identity is very much in the eye of the beholder. To seafood enthusiasts it's an elite oyster bar with good drinks. To cocktail geeks it's a rigorous bar with oysters. To scenesters it's a Brooklyn specialty spot with cool design. To summertime bon vivants it's a sunny garden with pretty cocktails.

Some people swallow an oyster whole; some people chew on it a bit first. I chewed on this oyster a great deal before at last the word *almanac* somehow came to mind. If you quote the Oxford University Press to point out that this book is not "an annual calendar containing important dates and statistical information such as astronomical data and tide tables," you are correct. Such were almanacs as they appeared for the couple of centuries following the first printed one in 1457.

As it evolved in the New World, however, the almanac, notes the *Encyclopedia Britannica*, developed into "a genuine form of folk literature containing, in addition to calendars and weather predictions, interesting statistics and facts, moral precepts and proverbs, medical advice and remedies, jokes, and even verse and fiction . . . [as well as] much incidental information that was instructive and entertaining." It seemed I could at least superficially borrow the concept to contain all the information I wanted to include but didn't know how to categorize in the book.

The attempt to wrangle all that is Maison Premiere ultimately proved impossible. Not done justice in this book are the breadth and quality of the food menu (including recipes) and the culinary minds behind it, the full extent of Krystof's wine vision, and the ever-fascinating and delicious local brews that circulate constantly through the beer taps. Nevertheless, given the challenges of organization, design, and maintaining focus and connection during an exceedingly tumultuous pandemic, I'm happy with how this came out.

Many places you might patronize might be stylish but lacking in food and drink. Conversely, many great culinary destinations aren't captivating spaces. Maison Premiere is one of those rare places that has both style and substance to a degree that's almost mind-boggling, given how difficult each is to pull off. We wanted the book to reflect that feat, while hoping that—as properly as it might settle onto your bookshelf—it would also look perfectly natural when observed on the fireplace mantel next to the antique phone, or at the end of the bar within Maison Premiere itself.

—*Jordan Mackay*

1.
THE PLACE

TO INCLUDE:

*before beginning; a failing bistro; beginning
again; meaningful geocultural influences; oyster
inspirations and design revelations; a crack team;
opening; of courtyards and horticulture*

G REAT SUCCESS REQUIRES ONLY A MODICUM OF OPPORTUNITY IF that opportunity is met with a sufficient degree of passion, talent, and hard work. Joshua Boissy, age twenty-two, discovered this when opportunity unexpectedly came calling one day in the form of a business card taped to the door of his Brooklyn apartment. The card belonged to a man named Jean-Pierre Marquet, pastry chef, entrepreneur, and owner of the lonely, failing restaurant Le Barricou, which happened to be right beneath Josh's apartment. The card said, "Call me."

Josh—at the time a waiter and part-time fashion model at Wilhelmina Models, struggling to make ends meet—hardly ever frequented Le Barricou and barely knew Jean-Pierre. They'd had only one conversation of any length, and it was about things like fly-fishing, restaurants, and industry stories of old New York. It was surprising, then, after Josh's call, when the two met to talk, that Jean-Pierre offered him the opportunity to buy out his existing managing partner in Le Barricou and become a new, better one.

Soon after, Josh passed all the money he had in the world—eight thousand dollars in cash, stored in a freezer bag—to the exiting partner. Jean-Pierre shook Josh's hand, passed him the keys to the restaurant, and walked out. Such was the beginning of Josh's career in restaurant ownership, management, and design. To appreciate the beginnings of Maison Premiere, one must first start with Le Barricou.

Art, Imagination, and Hustle

———

Josh grew up in Concord, New Hampshire, raised by a single mother who worked two jobs in hotels and restaurants to make ends meet. He was left to entertain himself a good bit of the time, which he would often spend in the woods, following his imagination wherever it took him. Though Josh and his brother never had much growing up, their mother possessed good taste and kept them in clothes that belied their modest situation, of which he was keenly aware because of the prestigious Concord prep schools that he didn't attend and the sprawling New England manors in which he didn't reside. From his teens, he worked two jobs and, with lawn mower and snowblower, hustled for cash when he could. Conscious of the fact that he didn't have a father or a mentor pointing him in the direction of culture or higher education, he gradually built a romanticized vision of a cultivated, sophisticated American life he aspired one day to lead. The first time he saw New York City was the day he moved there in 2006, at age twenty-one, in pursuit of the possibility of a career in modeling, and he met with some success, though restaurants would remain his destiny.

Josh met Krystof Zizka, his eventual cocreator of Maison Premiere, when they were both waiters in a cavernous restaurant-club in New York's meatpacking district. Krystof was raised in Philadelphia, the son of artists—theater directors who daringly emigrated from Eastern Bloc Czechoslovakia in 1977, the year Krystof was born. His parents worked all the time, so Krystof grew up in theaters. Even when he was very young, when he wasn't perched in the audience for plays or rehearsals, his parents would, in lieu of a babysitter, install him in the art-house movie theater next door, where he watched thousands of hours of classic cinema, from Chaplin to Kurosawa. His parents brought him along when they traveled, which was often, and, after the fall of communism, summers were spent back in Prague. After his parents' divorce, his relationship with his father grew distant. From an early age, Krystof was drawn to all manner of art and subcultures, from punk rock and skateboarding to hip-hop and film and food. Continuously since age fourteen, he relied upon restaurant work for pocket money. He ended up beginning a promising career in the music business at a Philadelphia studio before the potential of a record-label job took him to New York in 2002. By 2006 circumstances still found him working in restaurants, such as the one where he met Josh.

The two struck up a quick friendship, based on weekly dinners around New York, which Krystof—the older and more cultivated of the two—would curate based on his reading and monitoring of the current restaurant scene. These outings exposed Josh to types of food and drink he'd never experienced before, and he grew more complete as the world opened up before him. After work, the two also frequented the city's growing roster of craft-cocktail bars, as this was the early days of the cocktail renaissance and the dawn of the modern speakeasy.

Milk & Honey, the Flatiron Lounge, Little Branch, Employees Only, Pegu Club, Death & Co—the excitement inside these places was palpable. To go was to participate in the idea of bringing back quality cocktails, made with real ingredients, by people who were reviving the lost art of great bartending. The smell of citrus pervaded the air, as juices were squeezed to order and twists were peeled before you. The sound of new forms of ice—big, hard cubes cracking in shakers, crystal-clear blocks being shaved and chipped—created the percussive beat. Bartenders dressed in ties and suspenders, putting on a show while making clear that their profession was to be taken seriously. And customers stood by, avidly watching as their drinks were prepared in front of them.

Breathing Life into the Dead

———

Keys in hand, Josh suddenly found himself standing in Le Barricou wondering what had happened. He knew neither how to run nor manage a restaurant. He didn't know about taxes and fees and employment law or how to prepare a menu. There were three employees, of which he was one, and the other two worked in the kitchen and spoke a different language.

Growing up, Josh may have been short on culture, but he had a strong sense of self-reliance and was a natural autodidact. He immediately bought every book he could find on the bistros and brasseries of Paris. In his rare spare moments, he visited the best examples of the form in New York—Balthazar, Pastis, Bar Tabac, Café Noir—taking in the details, the chairs, the saltshakers, the frosted glass. He began to apply these observations to the dark, cold space of Le Barricou, turning it into the bistro it wanted to be—a homey neighborhood place with French character—along the way discovering his innate sense of design. Lamps and candles and chandeliers brightened dark corners, while mirrors expanded the space, and hard benches became banquettes. Josh worked on the restaurant's physical design first thing in the morning to when it opened for dinner at five, when he would become the only front-of-house worker, greeting guests, waiting tables, and bartending.

But the interior wasn't the only piece of Le Barricou's transformation. It had also been failing because it served uninspired product. As Josh threw himself into remaking Le Barricou's interior and running the restaurant, Krystof turned up and threw himself into helping his friend, who, he could see, was in over his head.

Krystof began to spend equally long hours as Josh at the restaurant. When Krystof first arrived he had been indulging a burgeoning interest in wine, but now he used his position as de facto sommelier to further his own wine education, reading up on French wines while conducting tasting after tasting with local importers. Already a craft beer aficionado, he turned Le Barricou's taps toward local brews instead of mass-produced, lackluster lagers. He revamped the coffee program, moving from industrial grounds to beans from an artisanal roaster. And the music! Krystof leveraged his industry-insider taste to create playlists of soul, indie rock, and jazz such that the sound alone beckoned passersby. Suddenly Le Barricou had transformed from a dank, generic bistro to one loaded with vibrant local food, good drink, an energetic spirit, and a cordial, cozy atmosphere.

When Josh took over, the revenue was a paltry, unsustainable five thousand dollars a week. After one year, when the revenue had grown to a million, Jean-Pierre joked that if Le Barricou ever hit two million in sales, he'd have to spring for lunch at Le Bernardin. Eight hundred dollars later, that three-hour Champagne-soaked meal was Josh's first experience of true fine dining. It also marked the beginning of the next phase, informed by what Josh and Krystof had learned: that the combination of meticulous design and rigorously curated product could result in great success.

A White Box

———

Buoyed by Le Barricou's rebirth, Jean-Pierre was keen to do another project. Josh reluctantly agreed, though insisted it had to include Krystof as partner. From early on, the idea was to create a Parisian-themed craft-cocktail bar.

Krystof found the Maison Premiere space in 2009. It was a disaster. Bedford Avenue in Williamsburg was faded and undistinguished, and a pit like this storefront, which had been on the market for ages, was a good indication of why. Over the facade of the 1890s building, a forbidding metal gate and cages over the windows protected a dark, filthy, crumbling interior. Jean-Pierre took one pitiless look at it and announced that this was craziness—it would cost an immense sum merely to turn this rubble into an empty white box.

Josh went back and looked at it a second time and talked to the building's owner. Eventually, he was able to negotiate an almost unheard-of long-term lease. One hundred and fifty thousand dollars and many months later, they were the proud renters of a white box on Bedford Avenue. Now it was time to figure out what this bar would be. At that time, there was no concept and there was no name. The thematic components that would become Maison Premiere came together organically, piece by piece, as if Josh and Krystof solved a jigsaw puzzle without knowledge of the completed image.

Horseshoes in Paris

From the outset, they weren't entirely without inspiration. They always had Paris, which became an object of fascination during the revitalization of Le Barricou and a potential theme for the new bar. Krystof had been there. And, shortly after taking over Le Barricou in 2008, Josh visited with Jean-Pierre for a bistro immersion tour. The transatlantic trip, Josh's first—in which even the Air France flight dazzled with a meal that included Champagne, metal cutlery, and a digestif—was a revelation.

He also came home with a shape branded in his mind—the horseshoe. This was the shape of the bar in a classic bistro they visited in Paris, Chez Janou. Josh's eye for detail was becoming more astute, and this bar, whose narrowness, compactness, and graceful curve would lodge itself in his mind, would emerge again as the shape of the bar at Maison Premiere.

The Old Absinthe House, New Orleans, La.

New Orleans

Alas, the Parisian theme wasn't to be. Searching through antique markets for the furniture and fittings he'd need, Josh found that the pieces he was drawn to were elusive and expensive. He was beginning to doubt his Parisian vision could be realized. Then things changed quickly.

Josh, pacing on the sidewalk outside Le Barricou, still remembers the phone call. Krystof, who had been buried in old cocktail books—including one from 1937 called *Famous New Orleans Drinks and How to Mix 'Em*—eagerly related his piercing intuition that their inspiration may lie in Louisiana at the end of the Mississippi River. Krystof described New Orleans's history, its deep entanglement with French culture, its unassailable cocktail pedigree, and its passion for art and music.

Within days, Josh was on a plane down to the Big Easy, by himself, with a camera. The moment he set foot in the French Quarter, he knew it was over. It was like stepping into a dream, like going back in time—the gas lamps flickering on cobblestone streets, live jazz reverberating out of long alleys, the narrow doors and old floors. Josh's creative mind was spinning, much like the slow rotations of the ceiling fans in almost every room.

One evening he spent at Arnaud's, the cocktail and fine dining institution in the French Quarter, drinking Sazeracs and French 75's elegantly made by bartenders in white jackets and black bow ties, smoking a cigar (indoors!), and marveling at details like the mosaic tile floors and burnished wood bar. Afterward, he stepped out onto Bienville Street, buzzed not just on booze and cigar smoke, but on New Orleans itself. Setting out to wander, he hadn't gone far before encountering his next revelation. Turning from Arnaud's onto Bourbon Street, his eye was caught by a line of people stretching down Iberville Street. It was an oyster bar, specifically Felix's Restaurant & Oyster Bar, one of two oyster institutions on the block (Acme Oyster House lies just across the street). Josh peered in the front window. He saw people crowded around the near end of the bar, where several shuckers were packed in tight, prying open oysters with the speed of poker dealers issuing cards while raucously entertaining the boisterous crowd. Farther down the bar, every stool was filled, and bartenders rattled shakers, foamed beers, and popped corks. He felt intoxicated just watching this scene.

On this trip and several others with Krystof, he visited all New Orleans's landmarks—Café du Monde, Commander's Palace, Old Absinthe House, Galatoire's Restaurant, Napoleon House. They were revelations for this twenty-three-year-old from New Hampshire. He soaked it all up with his eye and camera, aware of the tiny details that made each place visually profound to him: the sconces and doorframes, the patinas and chipped walls, the outfits of the employees, the china and glassware.

Coming back from these trips to New Orleans, Josh and Krystof had a very clear idea of what Maison Premiere should be—a New Orleans–inspired place with French styling, American craftsmanship, and influences from history. Paris was Josh's first love, but New Orleans even outstripped it because it was American. Since childhood,

Josh had always held a special fascination for American history and lore, but New Orleans's unabashed Francophilia and its idiosyncratic embrace of pleasure and joy showed him a facet of American culture unimaginable in New England and bridged a gap between history and art that led straight to Maison Premiere.

While he and Krystof knew they could build a place with great cocktails, New Orleans provided something they found lacking in the other outposts of the craft-cocktail revolution—narrative and context. These great cocktail bars existed in New York, but at the end of the day, their theme was only "craft cocktails." Krystof and Josh craved a narrative, a story to tell with their bar, and New Orleans gave them a framework.

Oysters of New York

Still radiant from his trip to New Orleans, Josh couldn't stop thinking about the lines outside the dueling oyster bars on Iberville Street, and the moment when he pressed his nose to the glass storefront and witnessed the oystery exuberance. His enthusiasm struck a chord with Krystof, who said, "We should do an oyster bar in the back. Do you think we can fit one?"

Vintage Krystof. Cool idea, but perhaps unrealistic? The room was already designed and the front-facing horseshoe bar finished. Nevertheless, Josh mentioned it to the designer, who surprisingly said yes, it could be done—but only a small, extremely compact oyster bar. So, almost on a whim, out went two banquettes, and in went a small oyster bar. And that quickly, Maison's identity changed.

It wasn't only in New Orleans that the mere presence of oysters produced energy and joy. Krystof and Josh had loved the whole milieu of the oyster bar since they met, visiting them often when off work. Eating oysters in New York just always seemed appropriate, a feeling confirmed when they read *The Big Oyster* by Mark Kurlansky, which had just been published and whose entire premise was "the history of New York oysters is a history of New York itself."

Immediately, they had to do two things. They had to suddenly create an oyster bar with the look and feel that would complement the horseshoe bar and other thematic elements. And they had to learn the oyster business, about which they knew nothing.

Absinthe

The other ingredient that made this unusual recipe work was absinthe, which on March 5, 2007, had become legally available in the United States for the first time in ninety-five years. An important milestone in the burgeoning craft-cocktail revival, the legalization of the revered but long-banned substance helped connect America's glorious cocktail past ever more sharply with the present moment.

When in charge of the bar at Le Barricou, Krystof had taken an interest in the notorious green spirit. As absinthes started appearing in the market, Krystof was doing the reading, learning from importers, tasting. Quintessentially French, absinthe was a perfect complement to Le Barricou's growing portfolio of Gallic wines and craft beverages. From the outset, Krystof bought as many high-quality bottles as he could get his hands on and even found a stand-alone absinthe fountain, which drips ice water into a glass of absinthe to dilute it. At one point, Le Barricou listed as many as thirteen absinthes atop its cocktail list, becoming—improbably, for an obscure Brooklyn bistro—perhaps the biggest adopter in the country.

Absinthe also connected strongly with historical New Orleans, as embodied in the Old Absinthe House. Even though it had devolved into a cheesy Bourbon Street party bar, the two-hundred-year-old institution remained—at least conceptually for Josh—a beacon. Mark Twain, Walt Whitman, and Oscar Wilde had drunk absinthe there. It was there General Andrew Jackson and the pirate Jean Lafitte agreed to team up to fight the British in the final battle of the War of 1812. And it is where Josh would gaze upon the remarkable, original marble absinthe fountain (at the time, gathering dust in a back room), which would stand in his mind as a totem before he replicated it at Maison Premiere.

With its herbal flavors, rituals, and history in the world of art and café culture, absinthe also connected powerfully to Paris. Chez Janou—that little bar into which Josh and Jean-Pierre had wandered in Paris—beyond its horseshoe bar, also is one of the world's premier absinthe joints. Josh still remembers the scent of anise hitting his nose as he walked in for the first time and the absinthe menu, some eighty bottles strong, and the towering glass wall of bottles anchoring the horseshoe bar—all of which would reappear in Maison.

No bar in America had chosen absinthe as a theme, and Josh and Krystof seized on this as another piece of the ready-made identity they claimed.

Building Maison

————

The thrift-store decorating job at Le Barricou would be but a simple trial run for the thought and work that would go into creating Maison Premiere. The detail involved in building out Maison leaped to the level of set design or dramaturgy.

Consider the storefront, which was modeled on old photos of New Orleans. They stuccoed over the building's original brick and gave it a historic lime-washed finish because they wanted the chipping and cracking to provide the feel of a hundred-and-twenty-year-old building. The hand-painted sign hanging above the narrow, unmarked door simply states "Bar Oysters" because, as Josh noted from old photographs, shop

signs advertised function, not brand name, as the latter would have had no meaning for the hordes of travelers passing through 1900s New Orleans.

Beneath the sign, the exceedingly (and somewhat uncomfortably) narrow mahogany front doors are based on colonial French architecture in the French Quarter. The bolts and hardware were bought from a company that makes new fittings for the US Capitol and the White House. Upon arrival, these shiny, lacquered brass bolts were sanded for hours and then chemically distressed with ammonia to create a patina.

The painting inside was done by an expert in historical re-creation who distressed the walls using up to twenty layers of various waxes and compounds to accrete a century of imagined history. He darkened the ceiling because tobacco would have been smoked inside. He patiently watched the path of sunlight across the interior and bleached the walls accordingly.

The floors are characteristic wide-plank yellow pine salvaged from an 1880s-era building and shipped from Louisiana. To emulate the decks of an old steamboat, where wood floors would need to flex, the Maison team used an ancient technique of filling the nail holes with cork and laying rope between the staves.

MAISON PREMIERE

Proper names are poetry in the raw.
Like all poetry they are untranslatable.
—W. H. Auden

Many people ask about the name Maison Premiere. So much meaning has been ascribed to those words—a place, a style, a history, labor, people, creation—that, as something uttered millions of times by all who work there, the name Maison Premiere has assumed titanic scale in our minds.

That said, the name is Krystof's creation. In the many hours spent trying to come up with a name for the bar, his mind ambled down the path of absinthe. The first commercial distiller of absinthe, in 1805 in the town of Pontarlier near France's border with Switzerland, was Maison Pernod Fils (later becoming Pernod-Fils, Pernod, and now Pernod Ricard).

Given that the word *maison* is French for "house" and *premiere* is an adjective meaning "first" in French (with the *e*, it's feminine; without, it's masculine), many people understandably take the name to mean "First House." However, this is not the case. Krystof simply imagined what another absinthe distiller might have been named and came up with the word *Premiere* as a surname, as in, say, Henri Premiere. (This turns out to be an uncommon name in France: one archival database shows only 885 people named Premiere since the seventeenth century.) Thus, Maison Premiere was the absinthe company of an imagined Pernod competitor, founded by someone named Premiere.

The name, though a fantasy, had a ring to it that Josh and Krystof immediately responded to. In short time it became an indelible part of the bar's identity.

Incidentally, absinthe infused even Maison Premiere's branding beyond the name. Its signature color of green permeates the sign outside the door, employees' business cards, and the website—and silhouettes of fennel, anise, and wormwood leaves line this book's pages.

Often in life and herein, you'll see Maison Premiere referred to just as "Maison," which is the diminutive everyone involved with the bar uses.

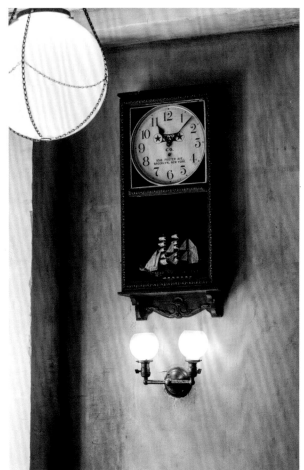

The art and artifacts are age appropriate. Paintings of Napoleon and Civil War forces were bought at antique fairs. Ceiling fans had to be specially rewired to rotate slowly enough, in the lazy, languorous pace one imagines of New Orleans. The old telephone dates to the 1920s and was connected when Maison opened, and it still may work, though it hasn't been used in several years. In the early days, it would piercingly ring all the time and annoyed everyone. Josh, however, thought it brilliant and said, "Too bad, just deal with it." Eventually customers started answering the phone, and it became a problem and was disconnected. The tiny, narrow bathrooms are reminiscent of rail travel, and the nickel-plated sinks were salvaged from an old train. The pull chains on the toilets work and date from exactly 1900. Procuring and installing these required tracking down an eccentric collector in Massachusetts with a warehouse full of ancient toilets and paying him for installation.

And the pièce de résistance is the replicated marble absinthe fountain, which Josh based on a few old, grainy photos of the Old Absinthe House in New Orleans and which required a small army of stone workers, welders, solderers, and plumbers to create. He looked all over for the green marble for the top, which he eventually found in Brooklyn. The base was made of soapstone. Then they needed drip spouts, which were more difficult to find than you'd imagine. You can't simply call up a plumbing store and ask for a tiny little spout that barely drips water. Eventually they found gas valves cast for factories and ordered a range of them until finding the right size. After being connected, the water first shot out in a torrent. To gradually slow the water down into a drip, plumbers had to connect ever smaller and smaller pipes, which were also directed through the bottom of the ice hamper, bringing it down to temperature. All this is capped by the bronze statue of Napoleon, which happens to be a replica of the one that sits atop the fountain at the Old Absinthe House, made by the same company, which Josh located after perhaps a hundred hours of internet sleuthing.

Napoleon House, New Orleans

Building a Team

———

Finding the first bar manager for Maison wasn't easy. In those days, more than today, serious bartenders had followings. The presence of a bar luminary generated an automatic base of rabid enthusiasts and reams of press. But finding one who would commit to an establishment created by neophytes with no reputation in the craft-cocktail world proved impossible. Josh and Krystof pursued several talented candidates and their protégés, but no one was willing to take the plunge. Eventually someone recommended a young up-and-comer from a Lower East Side outfit called Freemans, which had a reputation for cultivating new talent.

After getting in touch with the fellow, Krystof and Josh swung by Freemans unannounced to audition him. It could have gone better. Despite having a good bit of experience, the guy was nervous to perform and kept knocking over his tins. Not once, not twice, but a number of times, including into a woman's Gucci purse. It was like a slapstick comedy routine. But Krystof and Josh loved the guy's energy and personality, and they said to each other, "This is our guy! He's perfect for us." They hired him as Maison's first bar manager, where he earned the inescapable nickname Shaky Tins from his performance that night. That was Maxwell Britten, who would go on to be the highly successful opening bar manager.

Since Krystof and Josh shunned the spotlight, Britten—who was tall, charming, debonair, and, it turned out, congenitally clumsy—became the face of the operation to the media and world at large for the first few years. His persona, style, and bartending manner were perfect for Maison's introduction to the world.

Britten was charged with putting together a top-notch opening team of bartenders, and, inarguably, he succeeded. While Maison's lack of pedigree prevented it from luring established "bar stars," Britten's eye for talent would prove acute, as his hires helped put Maison Premiere on the map before they each went on to their own celebrated careers.

Natasha David came to Maison Premiere with experience at many restaurants and an acting background. She quickly gained a following in New York and in 2014 opened Nitecap, a renowned bar and industry hangout. (Sadly, Nitecap was forced to close in 2020 during the pandemic.)

Jillian Vose arrived at Maison via fine dining and then the Clover Club (another stalwart of the craft-cocktail revival). She was a commanding part of the opening team before leaving for a pinnacle position at Death & Co, where she rose to head bartender. Eventually she left there to join the team at the Dead Rabbit, the popular Irish bar.

Maksym Pazuniak had New Orleans credentials, where he worked at Cure. He had also coauthored a book called *Beta Cocktails*, which presented an irreverent, idiosyncratic approach to cocktails that prophetically delved into the bitter end of the spectrum. Pazuniak would go on to open a beloved bar, Jupiter Disco, in Bushwick, Brooklyn, in 2016.

Joshua (left) and Krystof in their office above Maison Premiere.

THE GARDEN OF EARTHLY DELIGHTS
Wherein Botanical Inspiration from New Orleans Becomes
One of Maison's Biggest Draws

For the first couple of years, Maison Premiere terminated at the rear of the building. Behind that back wall sat a vacant lot filled with mud and weeds surrounded by a chain-link fence. Eventually, growing demand for Maison's oysters and cocktails made it clear that the lot in the back should be exploited in some way.

So, Josh and Krystof went back to work. Outside of the French Quarter, the Garden District of New Orleans had made a huge impression on the pair. Josh had taken tours of the neighborhood multiple times, seduced by the dreamy lushness of the tropical flowers, creeping ivy, hanging Boston ferns, and flowering fruit trees. Stately, decorous balconies overlooked fountains and tile courtyards with pastel-painted wrought-iron garden furniture. What could be a more lovely setting in which to enjoy a cocktail? Josh and Krystof set out to recreate it in Williamsburg.

They turned salvaged timber from a Bushwick dumpster into a trellis. They replaced the chain-link fence with one wall of whitewashed concrete and one of brick. They built planter boxes from scrap wood. Josh rented a U-Haul and went antiquing in Maine, coming back with cast-iron urns from the 1800s. Old benches from the 1930s were bought from Central Park. The ugly metal door to the restaurant was replaced with French doors. A glass roof was constructed. Hand-painted Spanish tiles were laid. Cast-iron metalwork was found. A mahogany bar was installed. And dozens of varieties of plants were added in the spring: vines, palms, ivy, wisteria, ferns, flowers. Capturing the New Orleans Garden District to a tee, the Maison Premiere back garden became a cool, verdant respite from the steamy grip of a New York summer and, consequently, one of the toughest seats to get during the dog days. See Garden Cocktails (page 117) for some botanical inspiration from behind the bar.

William Elliott

On a visit back to his hometown of Tucson, Arizona, Britten discovered a like-minded soul in William Elliott, a young bartender who also played in bands and collected esoteric spirits. Given the opportunity to jump from regional obscurity onto one of the world's largest stages for cocktails, the young musician willingly relocated. Will ended up becoming Maison's head bartender in 2014, and since then he's been elevated to bar director and managing partner. While keeping some of the great cocktails of the past, Will has refined Maison's bar program over the years into something, substantively and performatively, unique in the bar world.

Oyster Bonanza

While Josh focused on the design of the room, Krystof spearheaded the oyster program. Krystof's love of curation and his innate drive to understand a category of product applied easily to the oyster world. During the weeks surrounding the opening, Krystof identified oysters that he loved and took note of the farms that produced them.

The plan was to have an oyster happy hour, selling shucked oysters for a dollar apiece. Economically, this is no easy feat, when the other goal is to outstrip all competitors in terms of quality. (Most dollar oysters are low quality.) To sell great oysters for cheap, he needed to buy directly from small farms. Cutting out all but the best distributors, he could provide high-quality oysters inexpensively, while ensuring better quality through shorter travel times. And shopping small farms allowed him to do his Krystof thing: stock the menu with cool, rare oysters you don't find at other places.

Obtaining certain brilliant oysters for Maison became a mission for Krystof, a holy grail, but it wasn't easy. Finding telephone numbers for many of the farmers proved a challenge in itself. And when reached, most of the typically gruff men and women who spend half their time damp and exposed in small boats in very cold waters had no interest in doing business with some nobody with a brand-new bar. Yet, every so often a cheer would erupt from Krystof's desk as he hung up the phone, when another small oyster farmer had agreed to play ball.

FOUNDATIONS OF MAISON-STYLE DESIGN

Here are the core design principles Josh and Krystof tend to follow:

HAVE A NARRATIVE • It's not enough to simply be "a bar" or "a restaurant." Find a theme—something that inspires you, instigates a sense of fun, and seems timely—and let it guide your choices. For Maison, they imagined "a place where Mark Twain and Andrew Jackson would have sat down for a cocktail."

DO YOUR RESEARCH • Maison was built on deep investigation into every relevant topic from nineteenth-century storefronts to New Orleans gardens to oysters to wines. Josh and Krystof are chronic bibliophiles, buying up every book on a subject. With keen eyes and mind, soak up every little detail about a topic. A mountain of tiny details becomes part of an identity.

CREATE MOOD BOARDS • A tool Josh and Krystof use a lot, the mood board is the place where those tiny details find a home. As they collect on a board and accrue connections among one another, these elements become powerful tools in seeing the bigger picture and understanding how to turn vision into reality.

FOLLOW THE RULES • When you create a narrative for your establishment, follow the rules it implies. Josh and Krystof's story held that Maison Premiere opened in the 1800s and stopped modernizing in the 1930s. As with any bar that's been around a long time, the twentieth century arrived bringing technologies like gas- and electric-powered clocks and lights. So, you'll see evolving technology—like gas lamps converted to use filament bulbs, an old telephone, slow-moving ceiling fans—up to the 1930s era, pushing a subtle realism that Maison Premiere had once evolved along with the world around it. To follow the rule, everything must work as it would've when new—even the woodstove, which was installed with a working chimney, though it has never been lit.

DIFFERENTIATE YOURSELF • Staking one's own claim in a world of imitators is hugely important. Don't do things just because they've worked elsewhere. Take a chance and do something different, as Maison did by featuring absinthe and offering lavishly garnished cocktails (at a time when minimalism was coming into fashion). Even if these things don't always produce huge revenues, the identity they confer in a crowded marketplace is difficult to understate.

ALWAYS USE QUALITY PRODUCTS • Never cut corners in terms of product. This includes the spirits—where even the well bottles are good quality—in the cocktails. The wine list, which is full of gems that would impress an oenophile. The oysters, which are obviously often hard to find and exceptional. And the food, which is rigorously sourced and prepared.

Opening and Beyond

———

Maison Premiere was a success from the day it opened in February 2011, as the cocktail renaissance was in full swing, and the buzz had been building in the weeks before it cracked open its narrow doors. Oysters were popular, too, and the shuckers were furiously shucking away. But when a rave *New York Times* review by Pete Wells came out, in which he completely comprehended the magnitude of Maison's creation, the lines began to form.

"Like Balthazar, Maison Premiere is a fake that sometimes improves on the original," he wrote. "At Maison Premiere, the set-dressing is taken to another plane. . . . So strong is the room's preindustrial pull that when you feel the urge to reach for your phone, you check yourself. Nobody wants to be the party crasher from the wrong century." And he recognized the quality of the product, too, noting that "stagecraft dominates the experience until the moment a plate of oysters shows up, and you eat one. That's when you understand that the fakers who run this place are for real."

The original concept for the bar was to have only a few oyster selections, but Maison ended up opening with eight. Within a couple of weeks, it was fifteen. And then it just exploded. Competitiveness ultimately drove the desire to have the biggest list in town. The only serious rival was the biggest of them all, the Grand Central Oyster Bar. But little Maison went toe-to-toe (with greater quality). Many days Josh or Krystof would place an anonymous call to Grand Central and ask the receptionist the suspiciously absurd question of how many oysters were on the list that day. The receptionist would say, "Please hold," and go to count. If Grand Central's total came back smaller than Maison's, the bar would howl in victory.

Ben Crispin, a front-of-house specialist, joined the staff six months after the restaurant's opening. Now general manager, he is a vital member of the team and a highly recognizable face of Maison Premiere.

In 2012, Maison improvised a tiny kitchen and hired a talented chef, Jared Stafford-Hill, with a fine-dining background. This changed the tenor of the restaurant, which evolved from an oyster house with plastic-wrapped oyster crackers to a place with monogrammed napkins and plates with a well-reviewed menu emphasizing elegant, innovative seafood. Stafford-Hill left the following year and was succeeded by his sous chef, Lisa Giffen, who put her stamp on the menu with inventive crudos and a show-stopping plateau de fruits de mer. Since her departure, the menu kept the best of her legacy, while digging deeper into New Orleans staples like gumbo, étouffée, and oysters Rockefeller. Of course, the menu will always feature spectacular, towering, teeming multitiered plateaux de fruits de mer, inspired by the opulence of Parisian brasseries.

In 2014 and again in 2015, Maison was nominated for the James Beard Award for Outstanding Bar Program. This recognition led to an even greater concentration of focus in all areas of the bar and resulted in a James Beard Award win in 2016, a crowning achievement for any bar.

Ben Crispin

PERSONAL STYLE AT MAISON

Despite the fact that the bartenders or managers you see at Maison are nattily dressed, a bent toward vintage fashion was never built into the concept. Indeed, a week before opening, Will Elliott remembers Josh saying, "Oh, jeez, I need to go buy a suit." Until then, he had worn almost exclusively chinos, sneakers, and button-up shirts. Now he's known for bespoke suits and handmade English shoes, while other staff members have fully dived into creating robust wardrobes of vintage clothing.

The escalation of dress at Maison happened early on, according to the unofficial custodian of Maison fashion, Ben Crispin, who has been at the restaurant almost from the beginning and is now general manager. According to Ben, the upping of the sartorial game began with himself and bartenders Maxwell Britten and Will Elliott leading the charge. This was fueled by a desire to better fit in and express the space. In this way, Maison has created its creators as much as they have created it.

No employee is required to collect vintage clothing, though many buy in at small levels. The "uniforms," if they could be called that, for bartenders are gray(ish) pants, a vest or suspenders or both (suspenders must be attached with buttons), and a bow tie or necktie in a vintage style. A lot of leeway is granted in every department. Managers wear suits, and Ben counsels many of them to have a few mix-and-matchable combinations of navy blazers and gray wool pants. For women, alas, there's no precedent for what they would have worn behind the bar in an early-twentieth-century establishment. They are welcome to wear vests and ties, but over the years, many have chosen to wear elegant, clean-lined, dark-colored dresses or skirts, and have kept long hair pulled back.

While there are many ways to participate sartorially in Maison's unwritten vintage culture, here Ben Crispin offers some helpful tips:

VINTAGE SHOPS • New York has some great vintage clothing shops, but so do many other cities. Check back often. New stock routinely cycles through the best of them, as people regularly clean out troves of vintage clothing. Ben is often able to buy pieces for fifty or sixty dollars that would have originally cost thousands.

TAILORING • When you find a good vintage piece, don't expect it to fit you perfectly off the rack. It was never supposed to. "Vintage suits were made to be taken apart and configured to fit the wearer, then put back together again," says Ben. "A great pleasure in wearing these garments is that they have been shaped to fit your own body."

VESTS • A staple of Maison dress, a vest is a very practical item. It can be worn with or without a jacket. It has handy pockets. And it needn't match the pants or jacket. Many great outfits can be created with contrasting vests.

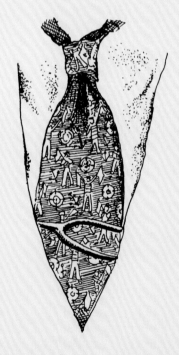

SUSPENDERS • Ben strongly pushes against clip-on suspenders. Everything else is buttoned, so Ben suggests employees have a tailor add suspender buttons to pants without them. Because the pants are suspended from your shoulders, not from the waist, you can wear them higher, where they're more comfortable—and they don't have to be as tight. Plus, they lengthen the legs.

TIES • Finding great vintage ties can be a lot of work. Modern ties can be recognized by bold plaid or stripe patterns, extreme narrowness, and an excess of shininess. Vintage designs will include club stripes or marks (bearing a regularly repeated crest or symbol), regimental stripes, or old paisley. Note that the tie width and lapel width should always be the same. Bow ties are welcomed (but not clip-on).

ARMBANDS/SLEEVE GARTERS • Some bartenders wear a band just above the elbow to collect loose material and keep the sleeves tight around the forearm, making it easier to work. Historically, shirts were standardized and sleeves were often too long for the average wearer. The band simply made it possible to wear these shirts but has become a staple of vintage bartender garb.

TIE KNOTS • People have become addicted to the in-your-face brashness of the large Windsor knot. But Ben loves the old four-in-hand, which is what boys were taught in Catholic school and what JFK and Fred Astaire wore. It's a smaller knot and easy to execute.

LAPEL PINS • Placed typically in the small slit on a blazer's lapel designed to hold a boutonniere, a lapel pin is a subtle display of ornamentation, which can simply be decorative or aesthetic or denote some sort of rank or organizational affiliation.

COLLAR BARS • Different from tie bars, collar bars have made a comeback in recent years. You'll see Daniel Craig wearing them as James Bond. A collar bar goes behind the tie knot to hold the ends of the collar together while pushing the knot forward. It gives a very tight, precise, secure look.

SHOES • In Maison Premiere, Ben likes the look of brown shoes, from dark brown to sand to maroon. He especially likes wing-tip shoes, preferably long-wing (where the perforated pattern wraps around the entire shoe), but short-wing works as well. Capped toes are fine (when there's a band across the front part of the shoe). For Ben, shoe polishing is an art, and he is a passionate supporter of Saphir polishes.

GROOMING • The services of a talented barber or hair stylist are essential. Maison is fortunate to exist right around the corner from Ludlow Blunt, the barbershop owned by Russell Manley. A progenitor of the retro-barbershop scene, Russell lovingly recreated a dazzling barbershop interior, which, coincidentally, would have coexisted in the same time frame as Maison Premiere. While men can come here and get a classic straight-razor shave, Ludlow Blunt serves all types. Indeed, Russell says, half of the clientele is women.

TIE BAR • The tie bar or tie clip is a handy thing, especially in a restaurant. It keeps the tie attached to the shirt, so it doesn't swing out and slap someone in the face or dip in a drink. It should be matched to the width of the tie, which should be matched to the width of the jacket's lapel. Vintage suits tend to warrant wider ties and tie bars.

2.
THE BAR &
ITS DRINKS

TO INCLUDE:

*a dossier of refined tools and advanced techniques;
a lexicon of Maison Premiere spirit selections and
outlooks; tableside preparations; a brief note on
a beer and a wine; the glory of Muscadet; and an
omnibus of cocktails, original and reimagined*

PRECIOUS FEW THINGS IN LIFE CREATE PLEASURE BY STIMULAT-
ing all the senses at once. From the clatter of the crackling ice in a shaker
to the fragrance of an herbaceous garnish to its tantalizingly tangy taste,
cool and captivating to the tongue, a fetching cocktail is one such thing.

Recognizing this, we aspire to incite joy through all means with every Maison
Premiere cocktail. In so doing, we embrace the grand, sometimes foolhardy gesture.
We shamelessly revel in the extravagant and rococo. And we employ arcane and esoteric ingredients. But when it's appropriate, we also celebrate the inherent beauty in
austerity and simplicity.

Every single gorgeous Maison Premiere cocktail is the product of many concur-
rent forces—unfettered creativity, meticulous selection of ingredients, deployment of
proper tools and equipment, rigorous polishing of technique and practice—all driven
by a relentless quest for deliciousness and an artistic eye toward presentation. Before
any drink reaches a customer's lips, each new recipe runs a gauntlet of reviews and
refinements.

In this chapter, you'll find a basic guide to Maison bar practice—including our
preferences in equipment—an introduction to our techniques, our opinions on spirits
and ingredients, and, of course, many recipes for both our original cocktails and our
particular takes on various standards.

The Maison Premiere Cocktail

_____

Maison Premiere delivers a highly refined cocktail. Some are garish and tropical; others are
suave and minimalistic. But each is constructed with exacting proportions and spec-
ified techniques. While every bartender is given some latitude to express his or her
own style and craft, we generally keep methods standardized to ensure a consistency
of product, no matter who is making the drink.

Of course, these things are less important to the home bartender. But we think it
best to at least explain the methods and choices behind each cocktail, so you can better
execute them at home.

MAISON TOOLS & TECHNIQUES

TO INCLUDE:

defining mise en place; shaking and stirring;
tins upon tins upon tins; suave moves for the
sophisticated bartender, and so on

Mise en Place

––––––––

The importance of mise en place to the culture of Maison Premiere bartending, and even to each cocktail itself, cannot be understated. A French phrase meaning "put in place," *mise en place* traditionally refers to the arrangement of common ingredients and tools at a cook's station in a professional kitchen. Of course, the idea carries far beyond a kitchen, though—a carpenter's tool belt or an artist's watercolor set, for instance, or a bartender's array of measurers, droppers, shakers, and spoons. The overarching rule is always the same: Place tools where you would intuitively reach for them while making a drink. Thus, all actions can be performed with economy and fluidity of motion.

For several reasons economy and fluidity of motion are especially crucial at Maison. First, space behind the bar is limited. Extremely limited. If it's a busy time, we may have two or even three people back there, and maneuvering is a challenge. Therefore, you can't be flailing about, clumsily reaching and grabbing for things you need. A tight, controlled mise en place keeps things organized in form.

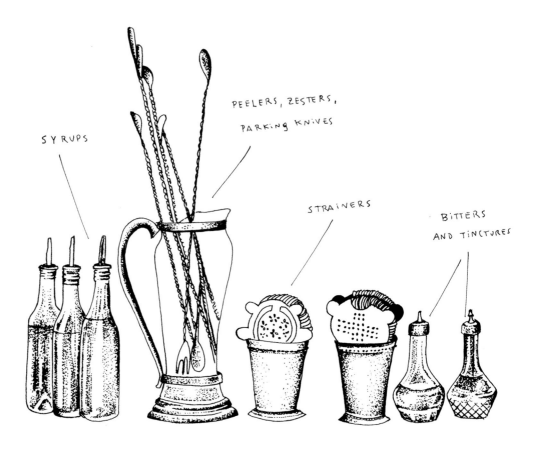

SYRUPS

PEELERS, ZESTERS, PARKING KNIVES

STRAINERS

BITTERS AND TINCTURES

Second, speed counts—not just on those busy nights but all the time; no one wants to wait long for a drink. A precise mise en place assists in that effort.

Last, we pay attention to that word *fluidity*. While efficiency is an important component of its meaning to us, so is a sense of grace. We endeavor to imbue the entire experience of a drink at Maison with a certain beauty and artfulness, which necessarily includes the bartender's actions and movements. Again, spastic lurching and clumsy carelessness are detriments to that effort, while poise and nimbleness contribute to it.

For the home bartender, the principles of mise en place apply just as well. Whether you're making a drink for yourself or for a group, the consistency, accuracy, and efficiency of your performance will improve greatly by keeping everything in its place. Funnily enough, so will your enjoyment of the drink. Just like a made bed or a cleaned room can add to the enjoyment of a space, respecting mise en place will ultimately result in a better and more enjoyable drink.

ELEMENTS OF MAISON MISE EN PLACE

*The mise en place for bartenders at Maison is to some degree dictated by the bar itself, includ-*ing the standardized placement of spirits in the well, the location of ice bins, sinks, and waste cans, and so on. However, the specifics of each bartender's station are left up to the individual to decide.

In this discussion, we won't refer to the well spirits or ice bins. However, the home bartender will want to consider these things when setting up. For instance, if making drinks for a few people, start with a bucket full of ice cubes, rather than opening the freezer and reaching into the ice drawer every time. And while you might not have a rail full of spirits at your disposal, consider pulling out and keeping close at hand all the ingredients you'll need before starting the drinks. These are simple, even obvious practices. But they make everything cleaner, swifter, and more organized, and it's surprising how often we forget them.

With that said, here's how a typical station at Maison Premiere is set up.

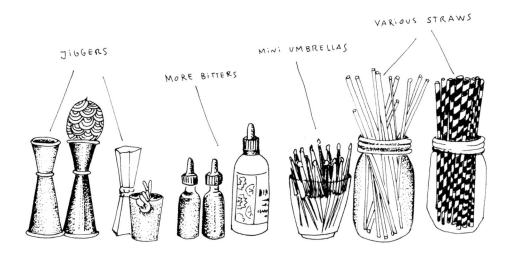

Equipment

———

Without question, serious bartenders obsessively focus on equipment, as do most committed practitioners of a craft. When it comes to shakers, strainers, jiggers, and more, everyone has unique preferences for materials, design, brand, and so on. Of course, none of these are crucial to the simple act of making a cocktail, which can be accomplished with even the most rudimentary of equipment. But if you take pride in your bar and stock the finest ingredients, it only makes sense that you care to use equipment that helps meet those goals.

At Maison, every bartender brings his or her own gear and sets up the bar more or less to their own specifications. Yet, over time, variations in style from bartender to bartender can result in some amount of drift, so in recent years an effort has been made to standardize a bit. So, here is the general "party line" on essential equipment. Since cocktail-making technique is inseparable from the equipment used, we've situated discussions of our basic techniques alongside the relevant tools.

MEET YOUR SHAKER

The shaker is the animating force of the bar. It creates much of the action, noise, motion, and energy that ultimately become the concoctions you imbibe. For these reasons, shakers are subjects of much discussion within the bar world.

Of course, seen from one perspective, the level of geekery surrounding shakers is a little absurd considering that almost any vessel bears the potential for mixing a drink, be it an empty soup container, a wine bottle, or an old can—all of which have no doubt been deployed for mixing drinks at one desperate time or another. However, given the centrality of these tools to all bartending, we'll delve a little more deeply into the discussion.

The modern approach to shaking was developed in the nineteenth century in America, when it was found that, if two vessels had mouths of different sizes, the smaller rim could fit inside the larger to create a seal, and a drink could be mixed much more vigorously to create textures and appearances hence unknown. The first patent for a shaker was approved in 1872, thus officially inscribing an object of eternal bartender fetish into the public record.

And rightly so. When the topic is precision, replicability, and speed, the conversation becomes more refined. In general, there are three major categories of cocktail shakers: the Boston shaker, the French (or Parisian) shaker, and the cobbler shaker. Variations of all styles proliferate. While at Maison Premiere we make no prescriptions as to what our bartenders use, there are a couple of consensus favorites.

BOSTON SHAKER • This is the classic combination of a clear pint mixing glass and a metal shaker tin, and it's the prototypical shaker used throughout the twentieth century. The advantages include that these are infinitely interchangeable in a bar setup

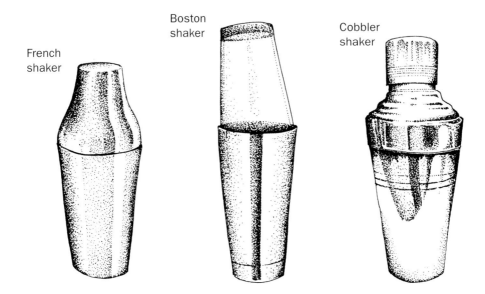

French shaker

Boston shaker

Cobbler shaker

and that the transparent pint glass allows both bartenders and customers to see what's going into the drink and how much.

In the days before measuring (aka jiggering) became standard, transparency before the customer was an asset. The Boston shaker can be used for shaking and stirring, giving it an efficient Swiss-Army-knife practicality.

However, this shaker has its drawbacks. Glass is an insulator and doesn't cool a drink as quickly as metal shakers. Also, pint glasses are heavy and unbalanced when nestled inside a light mixing tin. That can lead to accidents and muscle soreness for the bartender. Wet, heavy, slippery pint glasses being rapidly thrust back and forth in the wet hands of a bartender are a disaster (and lawsuit?) waiting to happen. Also, glass breaks, and probably every bartender has undergone the ordeal of melting an entire bin of ice during a busy service because of a shattered pint glass.

Finally—and this is neither a plus nor a minus, but depends on the desired outcome—the Boston shaker is marked with the protrusion of the pint glass's thick edge inside the tin, which creates a blunt interior notch that inevitably chips and crushes the ice. Now, ice will do that to itself anyway, but the added ice-breaking function of the Boston shaker must be considered.

Boston shakers may be ubiquitous—and we've even had some bartenders at Maison who use them—but generally we find them inelegant, clumsy, and encumbered by risks not worth taking.

FRENCH SHAKER • Also known as a Parisian shaker, this type of shaker must be mentioned, though it's not particularly relevant in American bars, largely because it never took off in this country. The French shaker is defined by two metal tins machined to fit seamlessly together in one tall, elegant, shiny obelisk. It offers the benefit of length and a smooth interior chamber that doesn't chip ice as a Boston shaker does.

The drawbacks have to do more with volume bartending than with craft, which is probably why the French shaker didn't catch on here. For one, the aerodynamic metal package is slick-looking, but it's also slick. That means for one-handed shaking (which Maison Premiere does not condone), it can be near impossible to grip with a single hand compared to the Boston shaker, which offers an exterior seam to anchor a finger. That slickness, exacerbated by exterior condensation and cold, can also make the French shaker hard to open. And finally, the greatest bugaboo of them all, despite the loveliness of form and so-called precision engineering, this two-part shaker often leaks, even after being "sealed."

French shakers are attractive objects and acceptable for home bartenders and as decor, but they lack in functionality and are not a good choice for the professional.

COBBLER SHAKER • A three-piece vessel patented in 1884, the cobbler shaker (named for the sherry cobbler, the dominant cocktail of its era) has enjoyed a renaissance in recent years. Some of this has been driven by its wholesale adoption by the bartenders of Japan, who dove deeply into the trade of bartending and ended up reflecting back to America its better qualities of integrity, meticulousness, and professionalism. The readoption of the cobbler shaker is fascinating, though, as until recently, it was considered more of an amateurish novelty than a professional's tool. Many American bartenders turn their noses up at cobbler shakers. However, since Maison Premiere's early days, we've embraced non-American bartending styles. And, thanks to the Japanese, the cobbler shaker became part of the tool kit.

If you've not previously studied the cobbler shaker, its design is unique. The cup for holding the ingredients is paired with a top, one end of which is a perforated, built-in strainer (though not a fine one). A third piece is a cap to fit over the strainer. Obviously, the cap is needed to seal the vessel while shaking a drink, but it can double as a measure. While cobbler shakers can be built to any shape or size, today's Japanese or Japanese-like models tend to take a more squat, wide form than the longer, narrower shape of French and Boston shakers.

Adherents of the cobbler, Maison Premiere bartenders among them, like the compact shape. We like the fact that it takes two hands to hold it while shaking, ensuring full attention and commitment. We feel it offers more control and nuance because of its limited capacity. And the rounded interior and shorter travel distance from top to bottom create a different dynamic for the ice cubes contained within, tending to round them off as opposed to shearing them. We also like the weight distribution of the shorter cobbler shakers, as well as the percussive sonic resonance of the ice slamming against the top and bottom during a shake.

Criticism of the cobbler centers around its perceived impracticality. Its three pieces mean more components to disassemble and keep track of. Annoyingly, after shaking the drink, removing the slippery, knobby cap can be a challenge due to suction created within the shaker. And critics will argue that there's no clear difference in the quality of the drinks that emerge from cobbler shakers. However, we contend that the sticking problem isn't a concern when using a superior brand of cobbler shaker (see page 52), which is so well machined as to separate easily when pulled.

A cobbler shaker is less efficient than a two-piece shaker. And a poorly made cobbler is a terrible annoyance. However, this is one of those points where we maintain that a little inefficiency here and there keeps bad habits in check and forces care and attention to be paid to the cocktail in hand. Plus, a little Japanese style in drink making is a beautiful thing.

BOSTON TINS · If none of the above ready-made formats completely win you over, the solution may lie in a sort of improvised variation adopted by many bartenders across the country: the Boston tin-on-tin combination. This setup is as it sounds: a variation on the classic Boston shaker but instead of a pint glass and a metal mixing cup, it uses two metal tins. This variation may have been exactly what early bartenders used in the nineteenth century before cobblers and French shakers were ever invented. However, the style was popularized starting in the early 2000s by renowned bartender Toby Maloney (then of Milk & Honey, now co-owner of Chicago's Violet Hour). Hence, sometimes these are referred to as Toby tins.

The virtues of tin-on-tin are numerous. Versatility is one advantage—tins of any size can be employed, so long as the aperture on one is smaller than the other. For instance, you can mimic the shorter action of a cobbler shaker by employing a short, stubby tin on one end. For another drink, you could simply swap that out in favor of something taller, to mimic a classic Boston shaker.

Another advantage is durability: Because each part is metal, fear of breakage isn't an issue; in fact, they can be used to scoop ice in a pinch (never ever use a pint glass for this). Unlike pint glasses, tins are efficiently stackable. And the durability extends beyond the equipment to the user—two tins are lighter than a Boston shaker, saving shoulders, elbows, and wrists from overexertion.

The final advantage is use. Unlike conventional Boston shakers, which can sometimes be difficult to pry apart (requiring an unpleasant pounding with the butt of the palm to dislodge or a coarse bang on the side of the bar), an all-metal shaker is pliable enough to require only a gentle squeeze to temporarily change its shape and break the seal. Also, the lower thermal mass of the metal cools your drinks faster than the higher-thermal-mass glass shaker does, giving you very cold drinks without overdilution.

Verdict: Perhaps the Boston tin is the ultimate answer to the shaker question, for both pros and home bartenders. Stackable, interchangeable tins offer flexibility, durability, and ease of use. While more utilitarian than stylish Parisian or cobbler shakers, Boston tins are less attractive as home decor but more practical and versatile as tools. And they're certainly less clunky than the classic Boston shaker.

MAISON'S RECOMMENDATION · As mentioned above, we do sanction the cobbler shaker, though we hold that our preference is also due to the specific use. That said, we love the tin-on-tin combination and use this method most frequently for shaken drinks. In choosing a shaker, strong stainless steel is important, so make sure you feel good about the materials. Most crucial is how well it seals. You want it to seal without force.

Our preference in tins boils down to two producers, whose equipment enjoys a vaunted reputation among professional bartenders: Vollrath and Koriko. Both make excellent tins. Though the former company is based in Wisconsin and the latter in Japan and it might be intuitive to purchase complete sets from one producer or the other, Maison Premiere prefers a mix—large Vollrath tins (28 ounce) paired with small Koriko tins (16 or 18 ounce), creating a deep-set seal with maximum internal surface area.

This combination seals with a simple twist and tap of one's palm, never to be bruised and scarred, pounded on a panicked drink rail, or boxed by brother tin sets. Unlocking them is as easy as pulling a heavy door open, with steady pressure and assurance of accumulated acquiescence. This combination also never requires any violence to either tin in order to lock, unlock, seal, unseal, or stay prone under duress.

As far as a cobbler shaker goes, there's one brand we favor, Yukiwa, with one particular line of tapered, angular Baron shakers that dominate the category. With brilliant detailing, state-of-the-art fittings, and vibrant acoustics, the Yukiwa Baron defines the Maison Premiere/American style. Because of its short, bulbous build and its weighted tins, the Yukiwa is easy to grip with control (a pleasure even) for a long, powerful, violent movement. When you shake with it, you really feel the energy your own body creates, which ultimately finds its way into the drink.

TO STIR, WITH LOVE: MIXING VESSELS

Bartenders debate which kind of vessel renders the best stirred drink. Some favor a metal container, which cools down rapidly, while others use glass, which absorbs more energy from its contents but is better insulated. The preference we observe the most is to use a prechilled glass pitcher, which keeps the drink cold and insulated.

The common styles of glass vessel for stirring are the straight-sided pitcher and the rounded, stemmed version that looks like a large goblet. Both work well. The former has become ubiquitous and for good reason. It's sturdy and durable. Its thick foundation keeps it anchored to a surface so it doesn't move while you're stirring. It can hold two to three drinks at once, and it looks lovely as bar light reflects off its crystalline etchings. However, the stemmed version is what we most often use. With its curvaceous shape, it's equally lovely. The stem allows it to be gripped without touching—and therefore warming—the vessel. And its tulip-shaped bowl permits a free, uninhibited swirl of ice and spirit. Either one works well. Just remember to prechill your mixing glass before stirring a drink.

STANDARD BAR TOOLS

JIGGERS • There are almost as many jiggers on the market as there are vodkas, and any one of them gets the job done. Some are functional but ugly. Others less functional but artful. We prefer a fusion of the two—functional and artful. Hence, we love a classic Japanese-style jigger. These have cups on both ends, each in different gradations: 1-ounce/2-ounce, 25-milliliter/50-milliliter, and others. For careful pourers, etched on the inside of the metal cup are bands signaling other fractional measurements. These jiggers come in two basic shapes. One is tall and narrow, and the other is wider and rounder, more of an hourglass shape. We prefer the former because we employ a move called double jiggering (see page 59), which is facilitated by the tall, slender jiggers and made impossible by the wide ones.

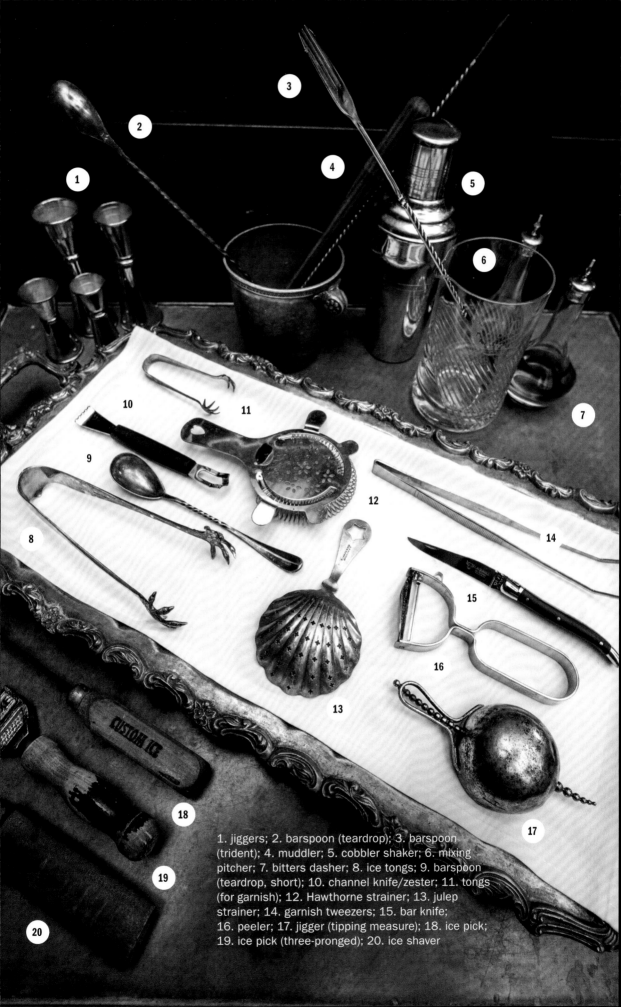

1. jiggers; 2. barspoon (teardrop); 3. barspoon (trident); 4. muddler; 5. cobbler shaker; 6. mixing pitcher; 7. bitters dasher; 8. ice tongs; 9. barspoon (teardrop, short); 10. channel knife/zester; 11. tongs (for garnish); 12. Hawthorne strainer; 13. julep strainer; 14. garnish tweezers; 15. bar knife; 16. peeler; 17. jigger (tipping measure); 18. ice pick; 19. ice pick (three-pronged); 20. ice shaver

STRAINERS · The cocktail strainer, a true bar essential, comes in two varieties: julep and Hawthorne. While you see both quite often, really only one is relevant to this book and to mixing cocktails in general: the Hawthorne strainer.

The julep strainer—known for its round, convex shape, circular holes, and graceful handle—is a classic, but has far less use these days than it once did. It came about in the nineteenth century when it was sometimes used for straining cocktails from glass to glass, but it was used even more as a substitute for a straw. With a fit that cleanly cups a julep glass, the strainer could be sipped through while keeping the solid contents of the julep—ice and mint leaves—from leaking out. Its simple, elegant design helped it regain popularity in the early days of the cocktail renaissance (mid-1990s through mid-2010s), when bartenders were looking for antiquarian flair (instead of, say, the horrid straining of drinks through the crack of two held mixing tins). And julep strainers do fit well into a pint glass, the favored mixing vessel until the current era. However, the aperture of a contemporary (cylindrical, etched) mixing pitcher as described earlier is too wide for a julep strainer, rendering the tool largely obsolete.

The Hawthorne strainer, invented in 1889, is dominant today. Its extending "ears" or "wings" give it the reach to fit over a range of different apertures, and the coiled spring allows it to nestle snugly within while providing an extra layer of straining. There's also a finger tab that provides the bartender intuitive control over the strainer, helping the hand maintain a firm grip while also giving precise control over the level of strain. These strainers excel at removing both ice shards and herbs. Also, for the deft handler, they provide an opportunity for split pouring one cocktail into two glasses—a show of bartender dexterity that is both efficient and never fails to delight. For the Hawthorne strainer, our choice is again Yukiwa.

BARSPOONS · Professional bartenders judge one another based on stirring ability—more on that later—though agility with a spoon is not dependent on the nature of the spoon but on the adroitness of its wielder.

Barspoons come in a variety of lengths, finishes, and detailing. Some are longer than others. Some have a coiled helix shaft, while others are smooth. The three major styles are: (1) tridents, which have a forked top end; (2) teardrops, topped by a slender beveled bell- or tear-shaped head; and (3) Hoffmans, named after the palatial Flatiron hotel, with a sort of shovel-like top curving slightly at the end.

When choosing the spoon for the job, it is nice to enjoy an array of options, in length and style, to accommodate various stirring vessels, ice types, and dilution rates. At the very least, you should have very short spoons to stir built-in-the-glass cocktails, as well as full-length spoons, large and weighty enough to push ice around a large-format mixing glass. Lighter-weight spoons, like tridents, are very nimble and quick with smaller, shorter mixing glasses, and heavier copper teardrops are better suited to negotiate the dozens of cubes in a mixing glass with ten tuxedos.

We advise bartenders, both professional and amateur, to keep a diversified quiver of spoons. The best tool for the job will intuitively become apparent once it's time to put it to use. At least make sure you have a long one and a short one, and choose among the options based on your own preferences for balance, feel, material, and implement.

EQUIPMENT MISCELLANY

Bartenders will want to have a number of other tools readily at their disposal.

ICE KNIVES · Used by Maison Premiere bartenders for provisioning ice, ice knives should have a steel blade, with a steel or plastic handle, and be easily sheathed and stored. In shape and style, paring and santoku knives are the ideal companions for the stylization of ice at Maison Premiere.

ICE TAPPER · Due to the advent of refrigerator ice and home cocktails, ice tappers were a mainstay in the martini-drenched 1950s and '60s. They enabled the user to crack and even smash cubed ice into their form of choice. To this day, an ice tapper proves to be a multifunctional bar tool, adding quick-and-ready dilution to a stirred cocktail as well as transforming machine-generated crushed ice.

LEWIS BAG AND MALLET · A Lewis bag is a well-built, closable canvas bag into which ice cubes can be placed and pulverized with a mallet until fragments of the desired size are achieved. A staple of nineteenth-century bars, this primitive device is still useful.

PEELERS AND GRATERS · Microplanes can be used to obtain fine shavings of citrus peel or spices like nutmeg. Vegetable peelers come in handy to create wide but thin strips of citrus peel for garnish or muddling.

MUDDLERS · Muddlers were more commonplace in the early days of the cocktail renaissance, as culinary sensibilities flooded the bar; some drinks—filled with fruit and vegetable matter—resembled smoothies as much as cocktails. Today they tend to be used with more delicacy, as elegance has come to be prized. That said, they're an essential tool both for, say, grinding the juice and pith out of a lime for a caipirinha and delicately tapping some mint leaves to express their oils in a mojito. Wooden ones generally provide a bit of tactile pleasure and sound better against glass.

FINE STRAINERS · When pouring a drink, a fine strainer (such as would be used for tea) can be held between the mixing tin and the empty glass to catch everything from offending bits of pulverized herb or pulp to fine ice shavings.

CHANNEL KNIVES · These knives are imperative for the aesthetic bartender, delivering dependable and stylized garnishes. The dual-purpose Messermeister five-prong zester/channel knife is our tool of choice. Both ends of the instrument play significant roles, with the channel knife cutting thick ropes of citrus skin and the five-prong zester ribboning the fruit, perfect for creating arcs and half-moons.

TONGS AND TWEEZERS · Essential for the elegant professional bartender and optional for the amateur, tongs are used for picking up ice cubes as well as garnishes.

What are tweezers but mini-tongs? They're good for strategically deploying small garnishes such as precut twists, sprigs of herbs, and various other sundries.

Techniques

Tools and ingredients are but two of the elements contributing to a superior cocktail. The third is technique. At Maison Premiere, we are exacting about technique.

As with actors on a stage, most of our bartenders' movements—from the way we lift a bottle off the shelf to the way we pour a drink—are studied, choreographed, and practiced. As we see it, classic American bartending is often boisterous and animated, with elbows-out masculinity. By comparison, traditions in Europe and Japan favor quietness, grace, and low impact. The latter style makes sense for Maison for a few reasons.

First, the area contained by our horseshoe bar is small. Not only is it somewhat difficult to access (you have to duck under a counter and through a narrow space—tough on broad-shouldered types), but, once there, maneuverability is limited, especially during busy times. When two or even three bartenders are back there knocking elbows while furiously putting out pristine cocktails, the challenge is working cleanly and efficiently without impinging on someone else's ability to do the same.

Second, much as economy of motion befits the sushi chef, sound technique supports the bartender. A bartender possessing self-assurance born of skill, dexterity, knowledge, and experience performs better. She'll be less stressed. Her drinks will be more consistent and more rapidly executed. Her manner will be lighter, putting customers at ease. All of this is anchored in good technique.

Last, and most important, experiencing a cocktail incorporates factors well beyond what you see, smell, and taste. Perhaps this is a holistic, Zen-like approach, but it's consistent with our belief in the eternal mingling of form and function. Enjoyment of anything depends on far more than the thing itself. At our bar, enjoyment begins with—a hopefully soothing but energizing—atmosphere. The bartender's friendly and courteous behavior also adds to one's pleasure, as does her proficiency in mixing a drink. Witnessing fluidity and grace as the cocktail comes to life stokes a customer's confidence that this well-made drink will deliver. Finally, once set before you and glistening in its glass, the finished cocktail itself is proof of all the time, thought, and artistry behind it.

In our internal bar manual, we have myriad protocols for bartender comportment and a long list of our preferred methods for handling almost everything behind the bar. But here we list a few of our most important techniques when it comes to mixing drinks. Mastering these skills will not only make you an advanced home bartender, it will give you a leg up on the professional!

JIGGERING

Not a dance step, jiggering is simply measuring ingredients using a jigger. It's a basic action few people think much about but is nevertheless crucial to accuracy, economy, and speed. Sasha Petraske, the late founder of seminal American bars like Milk & Honey, would famously put a piece of white paper under prospective hires' work surface just to test their dexterity and steadiness. Drops on the paper were strikes against. We don't go that far but do take measurement seriously at Maison, both for speed and consistency. But we also love a little panache, which is why we subscribe to a somewhat bygone technique known as double jiggering.

Not an even more complicated dance step, double jiggering is simply holding two double-sided jiggers simultaneously between the fingers of one hand. Given that the jiggers provide more than four different measurements (since each one can also be filled to the various fractions indicated within), this method promotes speed and fluency. Beyond that, it's a joy to watch, as manipulating two jiggers with the fingers of one hand is a skill not too distant from parlor tricks like rolling a quarter down one's knuckles or twirling a pen. Here's how it's done.

Before we begin, we train our bartenders to approach drink making with wrists facing up and open hands. That means when they pick up a bottle, it's from the neck, between two fingers of an upward-facing palm. Pouring the bottle involves a rounded, looping gesture to turn the bottle over. (Of course, this technique requires bottles capped with pour spouts to slow their discharge.)

Your other hand will hold two different-size Japanese-style jiggers. Most common is to keep a 1-ounce/2-ounce jigger between the index and middle fingers and a ½-ounce/¾-ounce jigger between the middle and ring fingers. These can be flipped from one end to the other quickly by using the thumb. The move is not quite as rapid a twirl as a baton. Rather, it's a slightly slower, two-step motion that anyone can do.

Practice and more practice will polish it into a quick and seamless maneuver that becomes second nature. We ask our trainees to wear these jiggers like rings. We tell them at the beginning of training that they should almost find themselves on their lunch or dinner breaks and realize "Oh, I still have my jiggers in my hand!"

This skill is almost archaic, given that at any time a bartender can simply adopt a single plastic, graduated measuring cup, which provides all the measurements in one simple tool. But plastic is so unattractive. And watching a skilled bartender deftly manipulate jiggers in one hand is mesmerizing, beautiful even. It's also efficient. And while double jiggering involves a bit of showmanship, it doesn't project the self-aggrandizing, attention-seeking of "flair" bartending. Sometimes economy can have its own flair.

SHAKING

Shaking a drink is not just a simple, violent act. Its purpose is fourfold: to chill, dilute, mix, and aerate the contents of the shaker. Different shaking methods produce different results. And, like our unique genetic codes, every person possesses a unique shake, which is why professionals tend to obsess and even evaluate each other by their shake. Qualities like grace, vigor, speed, and intensity tend to produce warm nods of approval.

Shaking fetishism reached its peak sometime in the last decade with a fixation on the so-called Japanese "hard shake," a technique developed by Japanese bartender Kazuo Uyeda using the cobbler shaker. For a hot moment, every serious pro in America was engrossed in mimicking the hard shake (which, ironically, isn't particularly hard but rather somewhat intricate in its efforts to push the ice throughout the shaker at different angles). It has a dance-like rhythm and requires a certain focus that gives bartenders a look of intense concentration while performing it, which has the effect of making each resulting cocktail seem more profound and serious—a good thing, largely.

However, we subscribe to none of this. We teach a few basic movements that work for our drinks, while recognizing that by default everyone's shake will be different thanks to the differences in our bodies.

While we care about aesthetics, we care even more about results. Luckily, our short repertoire of shakes runs the gamut. From vigorous to gentle, they all have a certain swagger while at the same time being acutely effective. With enough practice, each shake becomes natural and comfortably free-flowing, the exact attitude that produces the best drinks and most customer confidence.

We do have a few ironclad principles about shaking drinks, though. We never shake two separate drinks at the same time, one in each hand. Neither drink gets shaken properly, and, more crucial, it's dangerous. Failing to secure the shaker with two hands leaves a great risk of it splitting and coating all bystanders with a shower of sticky booze. Or, worse, it might slip out of the bartender's hand and strike an innocent bystander (we've seen this). Also, we never pound shakers, whether that's clacking the bottoms of two Boston tins together or pounding them on the side of the bar to loosen the seal after shaking. We don't tolerate pounding. Here are the essential Maison Premiere shaking styles:

THE MAISON "HARD" SHAKE • You could call it our version of the hard shake, but it's really nothing like the original except that it's done in a cobbler shaker. More violent than the hard shake, it's also simpler.

This shake calls for the cobbler shaker to make one full-size cocktail. The cobbler's compact size makes it essential here, allowing us to prioritize control and consistency. Adding the same amount of ice cubes each time while using the same shaking motion for a consistent length of time removes the variability using a larger shaker introduces.

Focused on dilution, chilling, and aeration, the Maison hard shake is used for drinks that could be served up (e.g., a daiquiri) and that lack any fat, protein, or vegetal matter (e.g., no cream, egg whites, or herbs). Protein and fat will swell in the shaker, creating pressure, while solid matter gums up the cobbler's built-in strainer. First, add the liquids to the shaker, then add ice to just shy of the top. Twist on the top half of the shaker and seal with the cap (always the final move, so that pressure is equalized inside the shaker).

Grasp the cap of the shaker with your dominant hand and the bottom of the shaker with your other hand, and cock the dominant hand back into the shoulder, as you might do with a shot put. Now drive it straight away from you in a flinging motion guided by your off hand and propelled by torque from subtly swiveling your shoulders. When almost at full extension, flick the wrist of the guiding hand and begin to pull the shaker back to your shoulder.

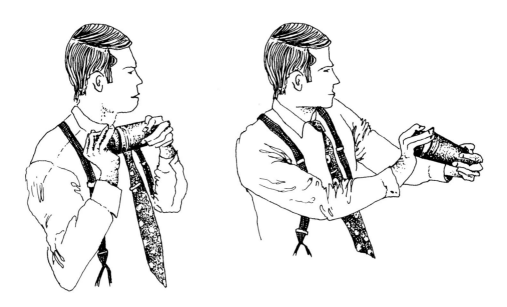

Repeating the action traces a narrow elliptical path with a whipsaw effect that snaps the ice from one end to the other. When to stop? Your own motion and vigor—as well as your taste—determine completion.

We don't advocate a standard duration for the shake but rather to use your senses. Feel the punch as the ice smacks the ends of the shaker. Note the timbre of the ice cracking within. What you're hearing is a very directional, focused chipping of ice. Repetition with the same amount of identical ice cubes and subsequent tasting will teach you the sound and feel of a cocktail at perfect dilution. Then you won't need a stopwatch; your body will calibrate through sound and feel.

One way to practice is with a bottle cap. Place a beer cap in a cobbler shaker and practice the motion, listening and feeling for its contact with the ends of the shaker. After a while, this shake will become second nature to you and you'll truly be able to taste the lovely way it enhances the body and texture of your drinks.

THE TIN-ON-TIN SHAKE • The Boston shaker style with two tins is a companion to the Maison hard shake. We use this when shaking greater volumes, as tin-on-tin can accommodate two, three, and sometimes four drinks at once. We also deploy it for all messy scenarios—egg drinks, fruit-containing drinks, or anything with mint or cucumber. These will all clog a cobbler shaker, not to mention that these ingredients take up more space in the shaker, too. So the greater volume of tin-on-tin is necessary.

First, ready the two individual metal shakers, with one being a smaller size than the other. Add the ingredients to the larger shaker, which will serve as the base, and fill with ice. Place the top shaker inside the base. The way to secure Boston tins is to slightly twist them while pulling toward your body, then, with the head of your hand (not with the butt of your hand, which can bruise) gently tap a few times with a light slapping sound.

The shape, weight, and size of the tin-on-tin require a different motion. This shake is done over the shoulder on a vertical path. Again, start with the small end of the tin held in the palm of your dominant hand, and cock it back up near the shoulder. Your other hand will hold on to the bottom end of the shaker. Now forcefully push the shaker back from just above the shoulder down to just in front of the abdomen, and then pull it back. Repeat until the sound and feel tell you you've achieved proper dilution. To loosen, twist and lightly squeeze the tins to break the seal.

One of our bestselling drinks, the Walcott Express, is shaken with a whole fistful of mint. When the shaker is packed to the top with ice, shaking it is an audible thing. At first, you hear a slow build as the mint mutes the ice. But as dilution occurs, the shaker picks up sound like a train gaining momentum until it climaxes as a piercing clatter. That's the power of the tin-on-tin. The Walcott Express is so physically demanding and people order so many that it makes our shoulders sore, which is why we cycle it on and off the menu periodically.

THE SHORT SHAKE • Less violent and dramatic than our other two basic shakes, the short shake is also quicker and not as hard on the body, making it a pleasant addition to the skill set. *Short* describes the distance the shaker travels, not its duration.

This shake serves several purposes. It's used for *dry* shakes—shakes without ice to agitate egg whites or cream into higher states of aeration, agitation, and foaminess. The short shake is also deployed for drinks calling for crushed ice, since it induces gentle melting and aeration. Overall, it's quiet and quick and—a rarity at Maison—performed one-handed.

The short shake calls for a tin-on-tin setup. Add the ingredients to the bottom shaker, seal the top, and pick it up with one hand. Place your index finger on the top half and anchor the butt of your hand against the crease where the two halves meet.

The motion is side-armed, taking place just above waist level, with a quick oscillation back and forth, letting the whip of a loose wrist generate the speed.

We allow this shake to be one-armed for a couple of reasons. One, it's difficult to achieve the quick back-and-forth whipping motion with both hands on the shaker. Two, since the ingredients for a gentle shake don't weigh much, the danger of the shaker slipping and hurting someone is low, especially with the action taking place at or beneath the level of the bar.

STIRRING

A well-executed stir is like focusing a camera. To achieve an in-focus, well-exposed photo, you align aperture, focal distance, and shutter speed. A proper stir depends on the alignment of speed, torque, and time to yield a superior drink. Imagine the crispness, clarity, and transparency of a perfectly stirred martini as a textbook shot from a Leica.

We stir a cocktail to cool and dilute it without aeration. After all, chilling and dilution can be accomplished much more quickly via shaking a drink, but that introduces air. A cocktail's consistency depends on how fast and how cleanly it's stirred. For instance, a cocktail will taste different from the hand of a bartender who stirs at 180 rpm than one who stirs at 90. Thus, it's essential, through practice and repetition, to develop a good stir.

Manual dexterity is required, but it can be learned. At Maison, we suggest starting with a long-handled barspoon and a mixing glass. The spoon's length creates a counterbalance, making it easier to spin the spoon when the glass is full of ice.

To learn to stir, practice with an empty mixing glass. Place the long spoon in the glass, grasping it just above the top of the glass. Hold it between the first and second joints of your ring and middle fingers with thumb and index finger lightly resting on the shaft to keep it in line. The point of holding the spoon down low is so the weight of the shaft above your hand generates momentum. For balance, keep your pinkie relaxed and out. Now, using your wrist and a subtle pumping of the arm, trace the interior rim of the glass just above the bottom with the back of the spoon. Rotate as smoothly and as rapidly as possible, keeping a very loose grasp of the spoon, allowing the shaft to revolve on its own. As you improve, the spoon's head will travel faster and more smoothly.

Now you're ready to practice with ice and liquid in the glass. The goal is to keep that motion smooth, not letting the head of the spoon lose contact with the glass and jostle the ice. As an old bartender adage says, the motion should feel so smooth and automatic that you could walk away and it would continue to stir.

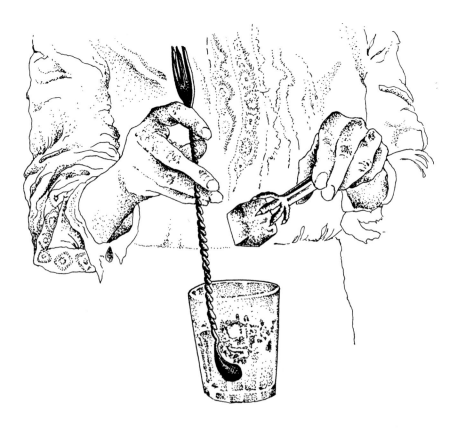

ADDING ICE WHILE STIRRING

You'll commonly see us add fresh ice to a cocktail as we stir it. This is because, especially using large Kold-Draft cubes, we simply can't fit enough ice into the mixing glass at once to rapidly achieve proper dilution and chill. Say the drink needs thirty cubes. Only twenty fit at once, so the others must be added as the ice melts. The only prerequisite here is a deft stirring motion you can set on autopilot as you multitask when adding the ice.

The mise en place here obviously includes a bucket of ice cubes, ready at hand. First, build your drink in the mixing glass. Then add enough ice to just exceed the surface of the liquid. Begin stirring. As the ice melts, the mixture loosens and the liquid level rises. Start to add ice rapidly, continuing to stir, adding the next cube when the mix slackens.

How to know when it's done? It depends on the drink. A drink served up, such as a martini, needs a full stir to be as cold as can be. However, a drink going over ice, such as a Vieux Carré, should be slightly underdone, as it will continue to dilute after serving.

STRAINING AND POURING

Straining and pouring are simultaneous actions, with a few techniques worth noting: fine straining, split pouring, and expressing a garnish while pouring. The first is common, while the other two are specialized moves rarely seen outside of Maison Premiere.

FINE STRAINING • Fine straining is as it sounds. Simply suspend a fine tea strainer with the nonpouring hand between the shaker and glass to catch debris you don't want floating like flotsam on the surface of the cocktail—anything from ice shards to tiny specks of mint to citrus pulp that might get caught between someone's teeth.

Just because, with a strainer, you can remove all particulate matter from a drink doesn't mean you should. For instance: daiquiris. We adamantly do not like a fine-strained daiquiri. Not interested in that velvety texture, we let the tiny shards pass into the glass.

Also, we don't always simply throw away the contents of the strainer. On certain occasions, we milk the discard for all it's worth. For instance, say you're making a buck—a cocktail in which citrus and ginger soda are mixed with a spirit. At Maison, we might fine strain from the shaker into the glass. Then we'll add the ginger soda, pouring over the top of the strained matter and into the drink. We do this to grab all the proteins from the ginger or herbs that help froth up the head of the drink.

SPLIT POURING • The act of pouring a divided stream into two glasses at once, split pouring is an advanced move that takes quite a bit of practice. Nevertheless, when mixing a double portion of a drink, it's an elegant gesture for the professional and home bartender alike. At Maison, the almost forgotten technique was revived and refined in the early days by Will Elliott. At the time, he often worked the service bar, where every second counts, cranking out drinks for customers not being served directly by bartenders. In the interest of efficiency and saving time, he discovered double pouring. However, the performative element of the move was not lost on him, and he began to train all bartenders on it.

Beyond showmanship, a qualitative reason for split pouring exists: it ensures the congruence of both cocktails poured from the same tin. To pour first one and then the other means the second cocktail was on ice a fraction longer and likely is more diluted. It's similar to pouring out one cup of coffee from a still-brewing pot. In the interest of being fastidious, a double pour eliminates the issue.

First, a few caveats. Split pouring can only be accomplished with a Hawthorne strainer with a divider at twelve o'clock. Second, it can only be done while pouring out of a thin-rimmed vessel. Thus, pint glasses and thick-sided mixing glasses are out, while tins and fine-edged mixing glasses are in. Third, if pouring out of a thin-sided mixing glass, do not use the spout. Orient the Hawthorne strainer so twelve o'clock is on any part of the lip of the mixing glass. Last, it works well only with fairly viscous liquids, so practicing with water is impossible.

Here's how it's done. Finish stirring, say, a martini. It's cold and perfectly diluted. Position two chilled glasses, lip to lip, before you. Place the Hawthorne strainer into the shaker or mixing glass (remember, not above the spout). With your finger on the tab, push the strainer forward to compress the spring, drawing the flat edge of the

strainer over the rim of the glass. Now invert the strainer so the liquid flows evenly but rapidly and is split by the divider at twelve o'clock.

Achieve further control by rocking the mixing glass clockwise and counterclockwise, like turning a steering wheel, allowing you to emphasize which glass receives the heavier flow to keep things even.

EXPRESSING A TWIST OVER THE STREAM

One final technique you'll see often at Maison Premiere and rarely at other bars is expressing a twist while pouring. Requiring no advanced skills, this is just a handy tool for making more fully integrated, multifaceted drinks.

Bartenders generally apply a twist to a drink after pouring it. (*Expressing* the twist simply means giving it a little squeeze to spray some of its essence over the cocktail.) This creates a powerful aromatic burst as well as little micropools of essential oils on the drink's surface.

While this works well enough, it leaves a little to be desired. The twist dominates the initial sips of the drink but not the latter ones. Second, after the first couple of sips, the oils from the twist are largely gone, meaning the subsequent portion is not really the same drink.

Therefore, we teach our bartenders to express the twist into the drink while pouring it. Hold the twist in one hand just above the top of the glass. Then pour the drink from a medium distance above the empty glass with the other, while squeezing the twist into the falling stream. This way, the essence of the twist becomes integrated into the drink. You can also discard the twist at this point, leaving nothing solid that the drinker would ultimately remove anyway, probably placing it untidily on the bar.

A NOTE ON THE UBIQUITOUS TWIST

It is a canonical teaching in bartending technique that, when a twist is called for, its essential oils are deftly wrung from the citrus peel, which is then dropped in the drink or lodged somewhere on the rim of the glass. When it comes to drinks served up, Maison Premiere sees this practice differently: We extract the oils of the zest over the drink—what we call "expressing the twist"—and then discard it. It does not go into the drink. We readily agree that the aromatic role of the twist is important. However, to leave it floating in the drink is awkward at best and, at worst, unsanitary. Addressing the first charge, a twist floating in a drink is inconvenient to the drinker: 99 percent of them end up on the bar, beside the empty glass. Additionally, it looks awkward. As to being unsanitary, well, we have no proof of that, but it leads one to ponder the care of the citrus. (For drinks served on the rocks, however, we do insert the twist, as it can be conveniently tucked behind the ice out of the way of the drinker's lips.)

THE MAISON PREMIERE SPIRITS LEXICON

Team Spirits: A Note on House Palate

———

As with any organization, the strong predilections of one or a few can easily be taken up by the organization at large. In bars and restaurants, this is called the house palate. As such, it is sacred to us, much as "company culture" is to a corporation or "team spirit" is to a sports outfit. Besides our cocktails, Maison's house palate is most clearly articulated by our bottles, be they spirits, wine, or beer.

At all times, we endeavor to maintain a large, but not sprawling, collection of bottles representing most categories in some capacity. Being inspired by absinthe, New Orleans, Paris, and New York, we naturally are well stocked in spirits that support those inclinations. But beyond that, our spirits menu differs from most others in the degree to which we carry and use in our cocktails obscure, small-production, and esoteric ingredients from around the world.

By nature (but not by rule), we tend to shy away from big corporate brands in favor of smaller, independent producers. This attitude was baked into our DNA from the beginning by Krystof. With a background in the music, theater, and art worlds, Krystof maintains a healthy skepticism of the market muscle and coercive power of big brands. He favors individual expression over mass appeal and unreservedly throws his considerable support behind the underdog against the market leaders. While, to some, a stance in support of the obscure, hidebound, and esoteric may seem like affectation ("you wouldn't have heard of the bands I listen to"), this is Krystof's unrepentant approach to life. Backed by endless research in service of thoroughly understanding a category, he takes every buying decision seriously and strives to get behind—for competitive advantage, for market differentiation, for independent spirit—things and people that have chosen to go their own route.

Since the beginning, Krystof imbued Maison Premiere with this orientation. Wine salespeople pushily repping the big, famous brands were swiftly shown the door, while the common bribes and incentives dangled by big spirit companies in exchange for stocking their products were reflexively rebuffed. Will, conveniently, grew up with the same mindset as Krystof. So when he eventually took over buying the spirits and the bar program overall, maintaining Maison's approach to its ethical, aesthetic, and substantive character was effortless and, indeed, a pleasure.

Since the earliest days, Krystof has been hands-off with the bar program, as it is entirely under Will's direction, representing his own tastes and fascinations. But Krystof's original independent vision—the vision they share—continues to guide the bar's culture in all matters of taste.

Spirits List, A to Z

ABSINTHE • *See pages 179–210.*

AGAVE—MEZCAL, SOTOL, TEQUILA • We adore agave but don't carry a huge selection. From the beginning, we were oriented toward high-quality unaged tequila, keeping on hand maybe one bottle of an aged version (*reposado* or *añejo*), as we are not particularly enamored with the flavor of oak-aged agave. Tequila as a category has been a bit dicey. In a market dominated by big corporate brands, fashion and celebrity plays, and shameless money grabs, one has to hunt to find authentic brands made by dedicated, artisanal growers that prioritize flavor—as is the Maison Premiere preference. Mezcal has been the antidote to the commoditization of tequila (though now big money has started to flow in, too), and in its elevation of small, individual, soulful producers, it still represents one of the great recent triumphs in the spirits world. Despite our enthusiastic support of the growing mezcal trade, for years we kept only one mezcal brand, and it was usually Del Maguey. But even though mezcal and tequila are not exactly signature spirits for Maison Premiere, we love this spirit so much that over time we've expanded our collection to include a handful of other small producers.

As for tequila, our well selection is often El Luchador. This overproofed pot still tequila, which isn't well known to the public, makes insanely good margaritas. For a tequila, it's got vibrant agave flavor and lots of heft.

AMARO • Taken as a shot after a large meal, amaro is indeed a great digestif. But since its inception, MP has used amaro primarily in cocktails, where it is a powerful ingredient that must be used carefully, because it can dominate a drink. We love the shading that even just a quarter ounce of these bitter herbal spirits can bring to a drink—tempering, say, the sweetness of a rum or whiskey or expanding the herbal profile of a gin. For a long time, you could get only a small spectrum of amari from light to dark, but now we can get regional amari representative of their places. We carry a few Fernets but also smaller amari producers such as Vittone, Vallet, and Angelico. An example of a cocktail featuring amaro is Future Days (page 142).

APERITIFS/QUINAS • This broad section can include fortified/aromatized wines and low-alcohol spirits and the once-obsolete category of quina (sometimes spelled *Kina* and short for *quinquina*). We are naturally attracted to all these things, given their niche quality, their European history, and their complex, bitter flavors that work so well in cocktails.

Aperitifs are generally low alcohol—i.e., lower than the standard 40 percent ABV common among spirits. They're often mixed with soda water or tonic for a spritzy afternoon or preprandial refreshment, though we use them liberally in all sorts of cocktails. A wide selection of aperitifs can be found on the market today—with new regional versions from Europe's alpine regions popping up with some regularity—and this is all to our delight. We play with a number of them and keep a rotating selection.

THE LITTLE BOTTLES

At every bartending station is an array of little dropper bottles—part of the mise en place, to be precise—containing all the bitters, extracts, and other solutions we use only in very small amounts (dashes, sprays, drops). Unlike other obsessive cocktail bars, we don't make our own bitters and extracts. This may seem a betrayal of the DIY spirit of Maison, and Brooklyn in general, but we have good reasons. One, we trust the outfits that make these things professionally to do a better job than we can with limited resources. Two—and this is the sacrilege—we do indeed believe that the impact of bitters in most drinks has been overstated. Substituting two dashes of one bitters makes far less of a difference in the taste of the final drink than does, say, choosing a different brand of spirit. Hence, we concentrate our efforts on the latter. Here's the lineup of little dropper bottles every Maison bartender keeps close at hand during service:

Angostura bitters

Angostura orange

Atomizers: absinthe, peated scotch, Reisetbauer carrot eau-de-vie

Bitter Truth aromatic bitters

Bitter Truth Creole bitters

Bittermens hopped grapefruit bitters

Bittermens mole bitters

Orange flower water

Peychaud's bitters

Rose flower water

Saline solution (page 176)

Vanilla extract

We love the intensely bitter and astringent flavor of gentian; hence we stock Suze, Salers, and Avèze. The first two are fairly intense, while Avèze is rounder and softer. We combine Salers and Avèze in the cocktail the Shining Path (page 131).

APPLE BRANDY • *See* Calvados.

BITTERS AND TINCTURES • We keep bitters like a chef keeps salt and ground pepper: always in arm's reach. Bitters are intensely concentrated infusions of botanical ingredients in high-proof alcohol, and are used to add aromatics and help mesh various elements in a cocktail. They're usually complex brews, flavored with a number of powerful botanicals along with some sort of bittering agents. Tinctures are similar in that alcohol is used to extract flavor, but they are typically just a single botanical. Tinctures provide a punch of a specific flavor, unlike the more evocative complexity of bitters. In general, we use bitters far more than tinctures.

When bartenders arrive at Maison Premiere to start their shifts, one of the first moves they make will be to line up their bitters. Anchoring the setup, square in the center of the station, will be a bottle of Angostura bitters, the most frequently used of them all. The other, less-used bitters and tinctures are kept in small dropper bottles. Angostura and Angostura orange are often right next to each other, as a couple of dashes of both are used in almost every house sour.

BOURBON • *See* Whiskey.

BRANDY—GRAPE SPIRITS, ARMAGNAC, COGNAC, BRANDY DE JEREZ • While not a huge category for us, these brown spirits do have a role to play at Maison Premiere. We always maintain a stock of Armagnac, Cognac, and Spanish brandy, aka brandy de Jerez, which is very good but a bit sweet.

At the time Maison opened, Armagnac was the most fashionable brandy. It's a haphazard wilderness of small family producers, full of soul, but it's also inconsistent compared to its more organized, corporatized, upscale neighbor, Cognac. But over time we really were drawn to Cognac for a level of refinement and finesse that Armagnac never quite seems to touch. Also, much Armagnac is, in our opinion, over-aged. It's great to be able to find old vintages to celebrate someone's birth year, but too many years in oak robs any spirit of its vitality.

Our go-to Armagnac, however, is Domaine Séailles, whose twenty-year is more complex and compelling than most Armagnacs twice that age. For Cognac, we love Février, a really zippy style. Others are Paul Beau and Guillon-Painturaud. In the case of Spanish brandy, which comes from sherry country, you can't beat Lustau.

CACHAÇA • *See* Rum.

CALVADOS • We are incredibly passionate about apple brandy. Aged Calvados brings a funky fermentative complexity that, beyond apple, hints at the richness of baked goods, brown butter, toffee, and crème brûlée. From the early days we were staunch advocates for the leading American brand, Laird's Bonded (which is uncut by a neutral spirit, as is Laird's Apple Brandy). Otherwise, American apple brandy is good but usually much more barrel dominant and often lacks the finesse and pure apple expression of Calvados. This is likely because we simply don't have the diversity and aged stock of apple varieties in the United States that the French have. But there's a growing interest in producing apple brandy in the US, and we're always on the lookout for local products.

CORDIALS • Concentrated expressions of a citrus made by macerating the fruit's peel in its juice and some sugar, cordials stand beside bitters and tinctures in the tool kit of Maison bartenders. We make cordials from a variety of citrus fruits—lemon, lime, and grapefruit, most commonly—and a quarter to half ounce can be found in a great number of our drinks, providing a stiff injection of intense flavor.

EAU-DE-VIE • At Maison this is a big spirit category, if not so much for the American spirits scene in general. This is because we simply love it—we push it, and we use it in a lot of cocktails. What is eau-de-vie? In fact, it's probably the highest expression of the distiller's art. Making eau-de-vie requires careful distilling of the fruit or vegetable itself, rather than simply adding flavor to a vat of neutral spirit. When done expertly, master distillers create spirits that capture a fruit multidimensionally, shockingly redolent not just of pear, say, but also of the leaves, flowers, and branches of the tree that bore the fruit. Reductively, it's just a better version of flavored vodka—Dolby surround sound compared to a tinny mono speaker. For that reason, we thought eau-de-vie could be a crossover hit nationally. Alas, it hasn't happened, except at MP, where many, many of our customers drink eau-de-vie cocktails. Its main challenge is that it's expensive to produce and therefore to buy. But we think the beauty in great eau-de-vie is worth the price. Specifically, we love Purkhart Pear Williams from Austria and Blume Marillen apricot. Hans Reisetbauer, also of Austria, makes a wide selection that we love. And Neversink Spirits, a local distiller, produces excellent New York pear and apple.

HERBAL LIQUEURS/ELIXIRS • We collectively use the name *elixirs* to describe the large category of herbal liqueurs. We call them that because so many of them originated as such—health tonics and medicines dating from more than a century and a half ago all the way to medieval times. Suffice to say, MP has a ton of these kinds of bottles, as their historical importance, botanical lineage, and overall peculiarity match our own fascination with all these things. Today their intense, complex flavors and unique mélange of bitter, herbal, and sweet play a prominent role in our cocktail program.

The category is a grab bag of herbal or medicinal spirits that could include genepy (*genepì* in Italian; *génépy* in French), herbal grappa, pastis, maraschino, gentian liqueur, kümmel, and so on. It's related to and often overlapping with aperitifs, amaro, quina, and vermouth, as they all draw generally from the same diverse bag of botanicals. Unlike those other spirits, elixirs are often higher proof, as you'll see in classics like Chartreuse. Higher levels of alcohol are able to contain greater herbal concentrations, hence the fiery heat of strong herbal spirits.

Some of our favorites in this category include an alpine genepy flavored with oregano, mint, and cinnamon, as well as wormwood. Sapin is an alpine liqueur mixing spices, herbs, and the signature ingredient of fir needles. Kümmel, a frequent

ingredient in several of the earliest cocktails on record, is a spice bomb flavored with caraway, cumin, and fennel. And, of course, Chartreuse, of the green and yellow varieties, is the famed tonic made by Carthusian monks from a 1605 recipe featuring 130 secret ingredients, including plants, flowers, herbs, and roots.

Pimm's, a Maison perennial, is a liqueur (and arguably an aperitif) based on gin but flavored with fruit and spices.

GIN • It's one of the foundations of the modern cocktail bar, but gin hasn't always been that way. Thanks to the craft-cocktail movement, in our time we've seen gin go from antiquated, unwanted liquor (in the days when vodka was king) to a spirit that's being reborn in myriad iterations all over the world by multinationals and small distillers alike. Gin's renaissance has been a glorious tale, and as a spirit it's a mainstay of Maison Premiere's bar program, which has an affinity for things historical, botanical, and powerfully flavorful.

When Maison opened, we keyed in on the classic styles of gin—Plymouth, London Dry, and Old Tom. But one could argue today that this dusty textbook categorization has broken down. Old Tom and sloe gins are not common and, as dictated by use, kind of their own category. Plymouth gin doesn't make much sense as a genre because it tautologically contains only one entrant: the always great Plymouth Gin. That leaves the remaining 99.9 percent of gins, which break down into roughly two styles: classic London Dry and modern.

Over the years, as we developed our style of drinks, we rotated an interesting cast of gins, while hewing to a full accounting of the classic taxonomy. However, today, if you look at the trends in our collection, you'll notice a growing appreciation of high-proof gins, also often referred to as "navy strength," because higher proofs can carry more flavor and intensity. We've also taken a shine to more gins on the "modern" spectrum—unique juniper spirits that nonetheless take gin in new directions. For example, a local product, Perry's Tot gin made by New York Distilling in Greenpoint, has a distinctive tarragon-forward profile that beguiled us from the beginning (it also slightly louches, or becomes cloudy when mixed with water) so much so that we had to find a place for it, even if it doesn't fit into any classic category.

Because we maintain a love of the historical, we often stick to five gins in our well. Thomas Dakin is a little-known British gin, based on a Manchester recipe dating to 1761. Our London Dry, it contains a bit of horseradish, a little spicy, savory note with very focused aromatics. Perry's Tot, mentioned above, is our navy strength gin. Valentine Distilling is our Old Tom gin, a style that's sweeter and simpler than London Dry; it goes into every Tom Collins. Mahon gin from the island of Menorca in Spain is our easygoing but pure Mediterranean gin. We call on this when a drink calls for gin, but it needs to integrate breezily with other ingredients. And finally, Plymouth, a rounded, pleasing, easy-to-drink gin with lots of flavor but not sharp at all.

LIQUEURS • A liqueur is a strong, sweet, flavored alcohol. That flavor can be anything from coffee to bubble gum. As a broad umbrella category, liqueurs are a bit hard to pin down, as they overlap with many other spirit families. For instance, an amaro is a bitter, herbal liqueur. Triple sec is an orange-flavored liqueur. Anisette or pastis is an anise-flavored liqueur. We use many of them as modifiers in cocktails and include a few of the old classics—e.g., Drambuie (honey-spiced scotch), Bénédictine, Strega, and Galliano (nonbitter herbal liqueurs).

PISCO · Technically nothing more than grape brandy, pisco gets its own entry because it's quite different from grape brandies like Cognac and Armagnac. It also has a long history in the US, first becoming popular in the West during the late nineteenth century, when ships would bring it up the coast from South America. Pisco comes from Peru and Chile—the two rivals battle over which is the true progenitor of the spirit—and is made from a handful of unique, often aromatic grapes. It is mostly bottled as an unaged, clear spirit. The best distillers, such as Capurro, which is the brand we tend to carry, usually offer several types. Acholado is a blend of grapes. And then there are single variety bottlings: quebranta, a workhorse grape, which isn't particularly aromatic; and the floral, aromatic varieties of torontel and moscatel.

Pisco Punch and Pisco Sour (page 174) are the traditional cocktails of the spirit. At Maison it has also popped up in various original creations over the years.

RUM, RHUM, CACHAÇA · A foundational category for us, rum was the first spirit group that we really got excited about. We found a lot of early identity in rum, especially as the garden drinks became part of us. Today, so many people associate rum with tropical fruits and tiki drinks and the Caribbean, it's easy to forget that, historically, it was all over New England and even made there from imported molasses. Likewise, New Orleans isn't thought of as a Caribbean town, but historically it was the American continent's gateway to the islands; hence rum played a large role there (as did whiskey, coming down the Mississippi, and brandy, coming across the Atlantic). The rum trade has a rich but tarnished past, making it solid historical fodder for us. Last and not least, it's a phenomenal spirit that can boast regional diversity, authenticity, and soul, as well as a multiplicity of styles with myriad applications in drinks. Rums are the foundation of our tropical drinks and don't play a huge role beyond that, though we do think it makes a wonderful spirit to drink neat and makes a terrific old fashioned.

From the beginning, we wanted to stock rums with provenance: rums that tasted like where they came from. At that time, the first real example was from Martinique, where it's called rhum agricole. This was a revelation, as the French style is to ferment and distill fresh cane juice—not molasses—giving the rum a vibrant, grassy, phenolic character on top of the sweetness of sugarcane. It's highly distinctive. Cachaça is the name for the Brazilian version of this. Rhum agricole brought us to a fascination with pot still rums—idiosyncratic, complex, often funky spirits from the Caribbean islands.

Rum was also one of the first categories in which we went deep on individual producers; that is, we stocked multiple expressions from a few producers rather than just one bottle from a broad swath of producers. This approach made it a little easier to grasp rum, because it's a sprawling, dizzying category with hundreds of producers, each usually offering a great number of expressions.

Of course, rum is usually thought of as a wood-aged spirit. And as much as aged rum is desirable, we also take a great interest in unaged or "white" rum. The dark spice and vanilla notes that come from barrels can cover up a lot of flaws in a rum, whereas the quality of the distillate cannot be obscured in a white rum. One of our favorites—and our frequent well rum—is White 'Stache by producer/importer Ed Hamilton. It's a blend of islands but is full of rich, flavorful esters of pure cane.

The regionality of rum is quite a draw. You can learn to recognize the styles of a particular place. From the grassiness of Martinique to the funkiness of Jamaican pot still to the smoldering intensity of Guyana to the light, airy style of Puerto Rico. We're still completely in love with the burgeoning industry in Haiti, where small producers with almost nothing put out some of the most revelatory distillates in the world.

SCOTCH • *See* Whiskey.

VERMOUTH • A fundamental cocktail ingredient, vermouth is a fortified, aromatized wine, which must contain wormwood as a bittering agent. While vermouth is a main-stay of everyday American classics like the martini and the Manhattan, we don't really have a vermouth culture in the United States like they do in Europe, where it is commonly consumed as an aperitif. Hence, for ages our vermouth options were severely limited to a handful of imports (Noilly Prat, Martini & Rossi, etc.). All that has changed in the last decade or so, as the classic cocktail movement has fomented a surge in European imports (there still aren't many domestic brands). For instance, in recent years, Spanish vermouths have burst on the scene. While many are similar in style to Italian vermouth, they do include distinctive and unique versions based on sherry.

VODKA • After a decade or more of hate showered down on vodka by craft-cocktail bar-tenders (an understandable reaction to vodka's insane popularity at the time, while gin was still an underdog), things seem to have settled down as the industry, and cocktail culture in general, has matured.

With regard to our menu, vodka doesn't play much of a role. But it would be nonetheless unjust if we didn't admit to the fact that vodka is sometimes our biggest seller. Now, with clear heads, we can actually admit that there is something to be said for vodka. We don't stock a lot of it, but we do carry vodkas made from potato, rye, wheat, and honey. And all of them are unique, expressing differences in weight, tex-ture, mouthfeel, and even aroma and flavor (despite the fact that vodka is supposed to have none).

We carry these because the most nuanced way to think about vodka is in terms of style, something which vodka drinkers are particularly attuned to. We try to check the various style boxes without feeling obligated to carry the big, obvious, go-to brands. We have nothing against these brands per se, but we don't want to lean on them just because of their popularity, when we can offer that spot on our menu to more interest-ing bottles that are more in line with Maison's character.

Our wheat vodka, Hans Reisetbauer's Axberg vodka from Austria, is quite neu-tral and clean. Chopin, a Polish vodka, represents the potato category and is appropri-ately rich and viscous and earthy. Barr Hill vodka is made from Vermont honey and is an outlier in the category, as it sports a fair bit of flavor, hovering between earthy and sweet, with honey overtones.

WHISKEY • Of course, whiskey is a massive category in the spirits world, but it's oddly minimal for Maison. It's not that we don't appreciate or respect whiskey; it just doesn't figure into many of our cocktails. That said, it's a diverse and growing category and also foundational to many classic American drinks.

We do care about it and how we choose and treat it in terms of classic cocktails. But whiskey cocktails aren't a fertile creative ground for us. The flavor profile of whiskey drinks—rich and somewhat sweet and spice-laden—just doesn't describe the Maison style. Plus, we happily make the classics—Sazeracs, old fashioneds, Vieux Carrés, boulevardiers—which seem to satisfy whiskey drinkers quite well. People who drink these tend to stick to them.

One reason we don't geek out on whiskey might be that it's not a particularly expressive category, meaning that the nature of individual whiskeys seems for the most part determined in the distillery and aging warehouse rather than the individual place where it's produced (with a few exceptions). That said, we stock whiskeys from Scotland, Tennessee, Kentucky, New York, England, Japan, and Ireland and look for examples that highlight those unique places.

Whisky from Scotland, spelled without an "e," is also known as scotch. We like the varieties from Campbeltown, the smallest and most obscure of the country's regions. The brands there are Springbank, Longrow, and Hazelburn. We also carry the peaty whiskies of Ardbeg for patrons with a palate for brine and smoke (one of the truly unique styles of whisky associated with its place).

In American whiskey we look for classic and balanced styles, so we like Wild Turkey and Russell's Reserve bourbon and rye. We also work substantially with Four Roses and Rare Breed, an overproof bourbon.

Japanese whiskey has become incredibly fashionable in the last decade, and it really is interesting. Japanese styles are modeled after scotch—so drier and earthier than American whiskeys—but they often do have a uniquely Japanese balance and delicacy. We love Hakushu, a lightly textured but bold-flavored whiskey. Also interesting is Ohishi, a rice whiskey that is incredibly light in body but has real whiskey flavor.

Tableside Cocktail Service

On our first visit to London's iconic redoubt of cocktail tradition, the Dukes Hotel, we found ourselves entranced by its tableside martini service. Having a drink prepared with flourish, ceremony, and intention right before your eyes somehow makes it taste even better, and we instantly wanted to be able to offer that feeling to our guests.

We would have loved to be able to stock an elegant bar cart with the equipment and ingredients for a single cocktail, wheel it over to the guest, and prepare it right on the spot. However, New York being what it is, there simply wasn't enough space in our floorplan to gracefully fit a bar cart. We instead developed a service involving two people, one to explain and mix the drink, the other to physically hold the tray of tools, glasses, and bottles.

However, you at home, hopefully, do not suffer the same spatial constraints that Maison Premiere does. If that's the case, we offer our tableside service format as a suggestion for your home. The idea is simple: procure a bar cart, preferably antique, and configure it specifically to produce a single cocktail (or several variations of one). A handsome bar cart is a perfect place to store your elegant cocktail equipment: an etched crystal mixing glass, a couple of long barspoons, Hawthorne and julep strainers, and an ice bucket. For cleanliness, keep a stack of beverage napkins. The lower shelf, if there is one, is a good place to store glassware.

Here we provide arrangements for the four cocktails we offer tableside. However, you can—and hopefully will—expand this rich concept to suit your preferences. You'll find that, whether for guests at a small gathering or simply for yourself, having the mise en place for a single cocktail arranged and waiting for you on a cart makes that drink all the more delicious.

SAZERAC SERVICE

The Sazerac lends itself well to tableside bar-cart service, as guests can be provided their choice of spirit—Cognac, rye, or bourbon—while staying true to the essential nature of the drink. Providing additional options of absinthe or pastis for rinsing the glass gives even more function to the cart, as does providing lemon or orange options for the twist.

Maison Sazerac service involves three tiers of Sazerac recipes, differentiated by rarity and cost of the spirits involved, and served in glassware of correspondingly ascending finery. We gave each version a name. The St. Jefferson Sazerac contains Wild Turkey 101 (chilled in freezer), Herbsaint 100 proof, Suze, Peychaud's bitters, anise, and Demerara simple syrup. The St. Tammany Sazerac involves Russell's Reserve rye, Jade 1901 absinthe, and Peychaud's bitters. And the top-tier St. Bernard Sazerac contains Maison Surrenne 1946 Grande Champagne Cognac, Esprit Edouard absinthe, and Peychaud's barrel-aged bitters.

We, of course, urge you to find and create your favorite combinations based on how you stock your bar cart.

BOTTLES
Cognac (one or two selections)
Rye (two or three selections)
Bourbon

EQUIPMENT AND GARNISH
Rocks glasses
Small glass for absinthe sidecar
Elegant barspoon
Julep strainer
Paring knife for cutting garnishes
Lemon
Bucket of ice

To mix the drink, follow our Sazerac recipe, page 112.

MARTINI SERVICE

At Maison Premiere, we serve our Old King Cole martini tableside with a floor manager explaining the drink while mixing it, as an assistant stands by holding the ingredients and equipment on a silver tray. At home, however, the martini is a perfect drink to arrange on a bar cart and mix for others. The gin and vermouth could be supplemented with other brands and styles to allow guests to choose and/or mix their own.

There is much talk of the ubiquitous dry martini of the '40s and '50s. The Old King Cole is that martini, containing only what amounts to several hard dashes of dry vermouth, as opposed to a fourth or fifth part. From Scotland, Old Raj gin is highly botanical and infused with saffron, which adds fragrance and a slight hue. At 55 percent alcohol, it is intensely overproof. The Castelvetrano olive is grown exclusively in western Sicily along the Belice River valley, near the town of Castelvetrano. To put it lightly, this is a composed martini—every ingredient and proportion has been carefully chosen to set this drink apart from any other martini at Maison Premiere.

We named this version of the martini for the painting of Old King Cole by Maxfield Parrish, commissioned in 1906 by American businessman John Jacob Astor IV for the bar of his Knickerbocker Hotel. At Broadway and 42nd Street, the hotel was a monument to prestige and opulence, becoming wildly popular for its luxurious restaurants and bars. One of the first iterations of the martini is said to have been invented there by head bartender Martini di Arma di Taggia in 1912, though historians speculate the original martini well predates this. Today—long after Astor's death on the *Titanic* and the shuttering (and reopening) of the Knickerbocker—the thirty-foot-long painting attracts crowds to the posh bar of the St. Regis hotel.

BOTTLES
Two or three different gins
Vodka
A couple of options of dry vermouth
Orange bitters

EQUIPMENT AND GARNISH
Mixing glass
2 or 3 barspoons
Chilled martini glasses
An elegant bucket full of ice
3 skewered Castelvetrano olives or an ornate
  container of olives
Tray of precut lemon twists (if entertaining) or a whole
  lemon with a channel knife

OLD KING COLE MARTINI

Prepare your mise en place first—skewer the olives and cut the lemon twist and have a chilled martini glass ready—because you don't want to waste a second between preparing the drink and pouring it into the glass.

    3 dashes of Angostura orange bitters
    ¼ ounce dry vermouth
    3 ounces Old Raj gin, stored in a freezer for at least
        12 hours
    Lemon twist
    3 olives

In a mixing glass, combine the bitters, vermouth, and gin. Fill the glass with ice. Continue adding ice as you stir until all the secondary ice has been submerged. Strain the mixture into the chilled martini glass, expressing the lemon twist with one hand over the stream as you're pouring the drink. Then place the lemon twist alongside three skewered olives on the sidecar.

TI' PUNCH SERVICE

Chacun prépare sa propre mort . . .

The ti' punch hails from the islands of the French Antilles (most famously, Martinique). To these islands, this drink is as culturally ubiquitous as the old fashioned is in America and Europe.

Simply described, it is but a basic yet soothingly addictive combination of rhum, lime, and sugar. Consumed in homes, bars, and restaurants, as well as at the beach, it's often treated as an aperitif (giving way to wine with dinner—after all, these Caribbean islands are official regions of France). However, you will find that it's infinitely sessionable, and an evening begun drinking ti' punch can often become a late night drinking ti' punch.

The French phrase at the top of this page translates as "each prepares their own death," wryly describing classic ti' punch service in which the host sets out rhum, syrup, limes, and glassware but leaves the actual preparation to the drinker, so that guests may construct a ti' punch to their own taste. This tradition perfectly suits tableside service.

Though traditionally ti' punch is served with unaged rhum, we offer a full selection of Rhum J.M aged expressions. Ask your guest to choose an expression and then a sweetener. We offer two: Rhum J.M Sirop de Canne, the reduced juice of pressed sugarcane; and Rhum J.M Shrubb Liqueur d'Orange, a rhum-based liqueur macerated with local oranges. Or, as is common in Martinique, you could simply offer a bowl of granulated raw cane sugar. Lime wedges are sliced thin, as only a couple of drops of juice, along with the oil from the peel, are added. Since the ti' punch predates the widespread supply of ice on the islands, ice is considered optional. Tradition serves the drink neat, but modern times often find the ti' punch cooled by a cube or two.

BOTTLES
Bottle of cane sugar syrup
A small selection of rhum agricoles, aged and unaged

EQUIPMENT AND GARNISH
Small tumblers or rocks glasses (ti' punches are
   small)
Glass containing barspoons and/or swizzle sticks
Limes or precut lime wedges
Paring knife
Bucket of ice

Add your preferred amount of syrup to the glass and then add 2 ounces of chosen rhum. Swizzle or stir. And then add a lime twist and ice cubes.

TODDY SERVICE

Nothing counteracts a chill like the cozy pleasure of a hot toddy. This former staple of autumn or winter is a simple, effective, and entirely underappreciated drink these days. The hot toddy's history is quite blurry. There are at least two major theories on the name's origin. It may have been repurposed during British colonial rule, as the term *toddy* refers to an Indian fermented palm, date, or coconut beverage. Or perhaps it refers to Robert Bentley Todd, a nineteenth-century doctor known to prescribe a warm mixture of brandy, cinnamon, sugar, and water for ailing patients. Today the hot toddy is quite synonymous with any hot cocktail involving spirit, lemon, sugar, and hot water.

Like the Sazerac on page 83, Maison toddy service is a choice-of-spirit offering, featuring our recommendations. Your bar cart should do the same by featuring your own choices. Along with the recommended spirits sit a bottle of aromatic bitters, ginger, Demerara sugar, and dashes of absinthe verte, as well as cinnamon sticks, star anise pods, cardamom seeds, and juniper berries. At Maison, hot water is brought in an elegant, antique silver pitcher, but any hot-water vessel will do. Our toddy is a very brief pour-over infusion—there's no steeping or concentration of flavor. Rather, it features the spirit, diluted with a subtly infused dose of hot water, gently sweetened and stirred. You'll find it is incredibly fortifying and delivers maximal inner comfort.

BOTTLES
Cognac
Bourbon
Rye
Aged rum
Bitters

EQUIPMENT AND GARNISH
Coffee cups and saucers
Kettle of hot water
Honey Syrup, Simple Syrup, or Ginger Syrup
  (pages 175 and 177)
Tea strainers
Tray of spices (including cinnamon sticks, star anise
  pods, cardamom seeds, and juniper berries)
Teaspoons
Lemon wedges
Fresh lemon juice, optional

Warm the mug with hot water, then discard. To the mug, add 2 ounces of your chosen spirit and the desired amount of selected sweetener (½ to 1 ounce is common). Fill the strainer with the desired spices and place the strainer over the mug. Pour hot water over the spices into the mug until full. Remove the strainer (reserving the spices for another use) and stir. Squeeze in fresh lemon juice, if desired.

WINE LIST: ON MUSCADET

Cocktails may get most of the attention at Maison, but wine lovers delight in the small but highly curated wine list. Foremost, it's a love letter to wines that pair well with oysters, featuring mostly white wines from northern France, which happen to be appropriately mineral, bracing, and saline—so obviously great with shellfish. Headlining the list, however, is a wine region that many people know of but few know much about: Muscadet. With more selections than practically any restaurant outside the Muscadet region, Maison Premiere gives this historically underrated wine a rare spotlight, honoring the fact that some—in France especially—consider it to be the best wine match for oysters.

THE MUSCADETAILS • For much of the twentieth century and earlier, Muscadet's reputation was as a generic, young, bland white sold cheaply by the glass in Paris bistros, where it was sipped mindlessly at lunch and paid no serious heed. Its sole claim to fame was as a complement to oysters, as Muscadet's citrusy acidity was akin to squeezing a lemon over the raw shellfish. But in the last several decades, the region has evolved. Better producers have shown that Muscadet can be an exciting wine on its own, with traits often ascribed to fine wines: the ability to express nuances of soil and climate and the capability of aging. While there is plenty of drab Muscadet in the world, there's more and more very good wine, which is still attractively inexpensive. These things together make it a wonderful restaurant wine. While Muscadet is taken more seriously than it was in previous decades, no one has championed it like the list at Maison Premiere.

THE WINE • Muscadet is a light, bone-dry white wine, greenish yellow to pale golden in color, with unremarkable flavors of citrus, apple, and pear and suggestions of salinity and rock dust.

LOCATION • The Muscadet region lies in the Pays Nantais, an area of western Brittany in the vicinity of the city of Nantes, at the mouth of the Loire on the Atlantic coast.

GRAPE • Many people assume Muscadet is the name of the grape, but it's just a synonym. The real name is *Melon de Bourgogne*, which, as its name suggests, hails from Burgundy, where it was banned from vineyards in the early eighteenth century when it was vanquished by grapes of greater character and quality, namely Chardonnay. Melon later found a home in Muscadet, where it appealed in part because of its resistance to cold weather.

CLIMATE • Being mere miles from the Atlantic Ocean gives this region maritime bona fides, making it mild and warm during the summer, cold in winter, and damp a good part of the year. The cool-to-moderate weather brings the wine its racy acidity and light texture. In hot vintages the grapes don't fare so well, losing acid and character.

SOILS • Across the entire region soils vary but are predominantly of gravel, sand, and clay with substrates of gneiss, schist, and granite. The ability to drain well, as these soils do, is essential given the dampness of the region.

APPELLATIONS • Muscadet has four appellations, but only one of real consequence. The basic Muscadet appellation covers the whole region, yet only 10 percent of wines bear this name. *Muscadet Coeaux de la Loire* is the most northern zone, where it is usually too cold to make great wine. *Muscadet Côtes de Grandlieu* is the westernmost area, a step up from Muscadet *ordinaire*. Finally, the largest and best appellation, *Muscadet Sèvre-et-Maine*, is named for the two Loire tributaries that run through it (the Sèvre and the Maine) and produces around 85 percent of all Muscadet. Protected from the chilling northwesterly winds by the city of Nantes, it's also home to the best vineyards, which lie on rolling hills and riverside escarpments. All of the selections at Maison Premiere are Muscadet Sèvre-et-Maine.

CRUS • A handful of charmed sites historically produce the region's best wines and have thus become recognized as *crus communaux*, or places whose wines are not generic Muscadet, but worthy of bearing a specific name. This name can then be printed on the label of wines grown there, so you know you're drinking something special. Since their ratification in 2011, the three original crus—Le Pallet, Clisson, and Gorges—were joined by seven more in 2019. The crus are determined by the quality of their terroir as reflected in the wines. For instance, Clisson, on a bedrock of granite, is known for wines of depth and longevity. Wines from Gorges are made from grapes grown on clay and quartz and are prized for their length. Le Pallet's subsoils of gneiss and mica schist are known to make generous, fruity wines of silky elegance.

VITICULTURE • Because of the cold and rain, producing ripe, healthy grapes here is a challenge. Muscadet's less-than-stellar historical reputation is largely due to this fact. But diligence, hard work, and talent can overcome tough conditions, and the producers who display those qualities tend to stand out. The Maison list highlights a few of these talented winemakers.

WINEMAKING • Given that the melon grape is rather neutral in character, the best producers employ certain winemaking techniques to make more expressive wines. Foremost among these is aging on the lees, where the wine is left in contact with the dead yeast cells that precipitate to the bottom of the tank after fermentation. This technique imparts to the wine a richer, creamier body and sometimes aromas of yeast or toast. Wines made like this are indicated with the words *sur lie* on the label.

TOP PRODUCERS • The Maison Muscadet list features several of the region's most talented producers. Domaine Luneau-Papin is an organic producer known for being one of the very few to bottle single-vineyard expressions of Muscadet. Maison Premiere offers several of these bottlings, including Clos des Allées, Terre de Pierre, and Vera Cruz. Another leading producer is Domaine de la Pépière, which also innovated in the realm of single-cru bottlings, of which Clos des Briords is the most famous. Maison's list also features a wine from the legendary Jo Landron, considered one of the founding producers of modern high-quality Muscadet, and a couple of wines made by his son, Manu (and wife, Marion), under the label Complemen'terre.

OYSTER + STOUT

Oysters just make everything better. Since the beginning, Maison's beer handles have been given to high-quality local, craft brews. Yet early on, the tap given to dark beer wasn't tilting as often as the others. The stout was stagnating. But oysters were flying off the shelf, so to speak. In 2013, Krystof agreed to collaborate on a beer with the local Barrier Brewing Co. of Long Island's south shore—a true oyster stout. Maison Premiere would supply the oyster shells and Barrier would turn them into dark gold.

The origins of oyster stout are murky at best but likely go back at least a couple of hundred years. After all, oysters were a staple food, and stouts (aka "stout porters"), one of the easiest beers to make and transport around the globe by the reach of the British Empire, were ubiquitous. Many people still swear by the combination of bivalve and brew. Perhaps it was inevitable that oysters ended up inside the beer vats themselves. Speculation has it that the first oysters might have been added for purposes of clarification, but today it's usually to add a hint of briny goodness.

For the first batch, Krystof insisted on using only shells from European flat oysters, aka Belons—the most assertively briny and metallic of all oysters. This worked well in the beer, but not so much for the staff, who were under enough pressure without having to separate out all the Belon shells. So future batches included a more democratic selection of shells. Can one taste a difference? Perhaps with the Belon shells, the stout is a bit more sharply saline. But even with conventional oyster shells, it's a briny, espresso-inflected, dry, incredibly silky beer that's an unusual but delicious match with its signature ingredient.

Maison Premiere Cocktails

———

Notes on Mixing:

- Boston tins and cobbler shakers are almost interchangeable for any shaken drinks, with a couple of exceptions. Cobblers can make only one drink at a time, while Boston tins are good for doubling or even tripling recipes. Never shake anything with protein—egg whites or dairy or any sort of fruit or veg—in the cobbler; always the Boston tin. For us, the Boston tin is the all-purpose shaker, while the cobbler is best for simple, three (or so) ingredient cocktails where precision and deep chill are desirable.

- Drinks recipes are listed from the smallest ingredient to the largest because that's how we always write the recipes for staff at Maison Premiere, in the interest of safety and efficiency. Bartenders must multitask, and mistakes will be made. When mixing a drink, it's better to realize a mistake after simply dashing in a few drops of bitters than after adding two ounces of an expensive base spirit.

- To keep them concentrated, drinks served over crushed ice don't get long shakes. This is because crushed ice melts quickly and rapidly dilutes the drink.

- A plus sign (+) in front of a measurement means to add the indicated amount plus a slight bit more. A minus sign (-) means to add just a tiny bit less than the indicated measurement.

- To express a twist is to "squeeze" it over the top of the drink. We often squeeze it over the stream of the drink as it's being poured from the mixing tin into the glass. The twist itself is then discarded for drinks served up and inserted in drinks served on the rocks. In the recipes that follow, when a twist is said to be discarded, the instruction is to express it and then not include in the drink. If it is not said to be discarded, include it in the drink or as instructed.

New Orleans Drinks

The spiritual and cultural inspiration behind Maison Premiere, New Orleans has also given us—and the world—many brilliant cocktail recipes, which we have nurtured, meditated upon, tinkered with, and ultimately made our own at Maison. All this with confidence that New Orleans gives us the thumbs-up. It's that kind of town; anyone can make a home there and claim a piece of it without coming close to changing its identity. Indeed, it's paradoxical to say of one of America's most historic cities, but to iterate is very New Orleans. We learned this and so many other valuable lessons from our New Orleans mentor, the barman extraordinaire Chris Hannah, formerly of Arnaud's French 75 Bar and now with his own two imperative destinations, Manolito and Jewel of the South.

À LA LOUISIANE

Hailing from the historic New Orleans restaurant La Louisiane, this spiritous cocktail is a less vaunted member of the Southern cocktail canon and contains many liquid tropes of New Orleans drinking: Peychaud's bitters, a touch of absinthe, and rye whiskey (all chiefly associated with the Sazerac); Bénédictine (notable in the Vieux Carré); and red vermouth (relating it to its northern neighbor, the Manhattan). Due to the precision required in balancing it through proper measurement, the À la Louisiane has long been a litmus test cocktail in the training of all Maison Premiere bartenders, alongside more prominent names such as the martini and the daiquiri. The recipe was first printed in the 1938 classic *New Orleans Drinks and How to Mix 'Em*.

    5 dashes of La Muse Verte absinthe
    5 dashes of Peychaud's bitters
    ½ ounce Bénédictine
    ¾ ounce La Quintinye Rouge vermouth
    1¾ ounces Wild Turkey 101 rye whiskey
    Skewered candied cherry, for garnish

In a mixing glass, combine the absinthe, bitters, Bénédictine, vermouth, and rye, and then fill with ice. Stir the mixture rapidly to chill and strain into a chilled Nick & Nora glass. Garnish with a skewered candied cherry.

ARNAUD'S FRENCH 75

While the French 75 has become a global classic when made with gin, we enjoy (and adhere to) the original recipe which employs Cognac, giving the drink breadth and a soothing richness that doesn't appear in the gin version. Arnaud's French 75 Bar is one of the great New Orleans institutions, and this is similar to how the drink is made there. When we first featured our version at Maison Premiere, we took great care to amplify flavor while preserving its simplicity by employing higher-grade ingredients than you'll find in standard versions in New Orleans—small-grower Champagne instead of an industrial sparkling wine, artisanal Cognac instead of less-expressive brandy from the large houses—combined with a little fresh lemon juice and Demerara simple syrup. Word to the wise: When making this drink at home, use a wineglass (not a flute); pour the Champagne into the glass first; then pour the shaken mixture of Cognac, lemon, and sugar on top of the Champagne. Finish with a lemon twist, and inhale before your first sip.

¼ ounce Simple Syrup (page 175)
¼ ounce lemon juice
1 ounce Dudognon VSOP Cognac
3½ ounces Champagne
Expressed lemon twist, for garnish

To a Boston tin or cobbler shaker, add the simple syrup, lemon juice, and Cognac. Fill the shaker with ice, cover, and shake vigorously but briefly—5 to 10 seconds. Add the Champagne to a small white wine glass and then fine strain the shaker contents into the glass. Garnish with an expressed lemon twist balanced on the lip of the glass.

OLD HICKORY

Cocktail lore has it that the old hickory was a favorite of the future president of the United States, Andrew Jackson, while he was stationed in New Orleans in the 1810s. Despite its namesake's tough-as-nails reputation for swagger and brawling, this cocktail is smooth and easy, both to prepare and to sip. Also, its format can accommodate any variety of different fortified wines; simply combine a dry fortified wine with a sweet one, and add a few dashes of bitters and a citrus twist. While this pleasurable but mellow low-ABV concoction might not induce the full-throated boldness of a whiskey drink, that can often be for the best.

> 4 dashes of Peychaud's bitters
> 4 dashes of orange bitters
> 1 ounce Dolin dry vermouth
> 1½ ounces La Quintinye Rouge vermouth
> Orange twist, for garnish

In a rocks glass, combine the Peychaud's bitters, orange bitters, dry vermouth, and red vermouth, then top with ice. Briefly stir the mixture until the glass starts to sweat. Serve with an expressed and inserted orange twist.

CARONDELET

One of our most frequently ordered drinks, the Carondelet is built on the flavor template of a Ramos gin fizz—the notoriously laborious New Orleans classic—but artfully reimagined without the dairy and egg white. Its success includes several Ramos features as well as a few new ones: equal parts lemon and lime juice, orange flower water, and vanilla (all of which appear in the classic Ramos), as well as a salted honey syrup instead of simple syrup as a sweetener. Named for a famous eastbound street in New Orleans, the cocktail has broad appeal that makes it easy to look past its nuance and swagger. This is a cocktail that can do no wrong. It never offends but is also never forgettable. It is never the season's quintessential drink, but it is always in season. It is enjoyed by first-time cocktail drinkers and consummate NYC barflies alike.

½ ounce lemon juice
½ ounce lime juice
¾ ounce Carondelet Syrup (recipe follows)
2 ounces Hayman's London Dry gin

In a Boston tin shaker, add the lemon and lime juices, Carondelet syrup, and gin. Fill the shaker with ice, cover, and shake vigorously for 20 seconds. Fine strain the liquid into a chilled coupe.

CARONDELET SYRUP

1 cup water
1 cup orange blossom honey
5 pinches of Maldon salt
2 dashes of orange flower water
2 dashes of Madagascar vanilla extract

In a small saucepan over medium-high heat, bring the water to a low simmer. Add the honey and stir until the honey and water are combined. Then add the salt, orange flower water, and vanilla extract and stir until dissolved. Allow the mixture to cool before using.

HURRICANE

We reclaimed this fruity, rum-based refresher from the depths of depravity, cutting against the pretense of the New York craft-cocktail scene (which would never stoop to list such a drink) by prominently placing it on our opening menu, and taking great care in its tasteful recreation. Currently, in New Orleans, the hurricane is nothing more than sickly-sweet, high-octane fuel of fratty Bourbon Street debauchery, poured like Icees from swirling machines into supersize plastic cups and carried around by partiers. However, despite its loucheness, the drink does possess classical roots and is indisputably a staple of the city we revere. So we resurrected it by serving it on crushed ice with two opposing straws (to facilitate sharing), employing a pot still Jamaican rum—a far superior choice to the bland white rums used in the French Quarter—and recreating its original base, a product called fassionola (a red-colored fruit punch concentrate of the 1930s), as a delicious amalgam of fresh passion fruit puree blended with coconut and homemade grenadine. And while this has never been a top seller, we think it was one of the gateway tropical drinks that led to the resurgence of interest in tiki and tropical drinks in the revivalist bar scene of early 2010s New York and abroad. Our version is adapted from the 1940s recipe of the mainstay New Orleans bar Pat O'Brien's.

    1 ounce lemon juice
    1 ounce Passion Fruit Syrup (page 177)
    1 ounce Appleton V/X rum
    1 ounce Rhum J.M Blanc
    2 large straws, for garnish

In a hurricane glass, add the lemon juice, passion fruit syrup, and rums. Insert a swizzle stick and fill the glass with crushed ice over the swizzle stick. Agitate gently with the swizzle for about 15 seconds, then remove it carefully. Add more crushed ice over the top and garnish with two opposing large straws.

RAMOS GIN FIZZ

The Ramos gin fizz is one of the most iconic New Orleans cocktails, perhaps second only to the Sazerac. Its charms are irresistible: lemon and lime provide the citric electricity over the low herbal hum of the gin, while cream, vanilla, and egg white give it a velvety, dessert-like richness, and the final addition of soda water sends the froth literally over the top. It's a brilliant concoction, often served at brunch or during the daytime, but delicious and appropriate any time you need a lift.

Because it's so labor intensive, many bars have rules regarding when and how many RGFs one can order. At Maison Premiere, however, we encourage our guests to order the Ramos, and many of our bartenders enjoy the performative aspect to producing this labor of love. Our version has been tweaked and obsessed over until it matured into this exact recipe. You'll note an excessive amount of shaking, including shaking until two ice cubes have completely dissolved into the drink. We do this because, though you could shake this drink in a tin full of ice and achieve cooling and dilution faster, that way risks overdilution. Additionally, the ice cubes remaining in the tin tend to trap and freeze some of the desirable froth we want to see end up in the glass. So instead we add a small amount of ice and shake until it dissolves.

3 drops of vanilla extract

6 drops of orange flower water

3 dashes of Angostura orange bitters

+½ ounce lemon juice

+½ ounce lime juice

1 ounce Simple Syrup (page 175)

2 ounces Plymouth gin

1 ounce heavy cream

1 egg white

2 lemon twists, for expressing

2–3 ounces fresh soda water, as highly carbonated as possible

In a Boston tin shaker, combine the vanilla extract, orange flower water, bitters, lemon juice, lime juice, simple syrup, and gin. Add the cream and dry shake vigorously for about 10 seconds. Then add the egg white and shake again for 10 to 15 seconds. Now open the shaker and add two medium-to-large cubes of ice, seal the shaker, and shake it all together until the ice cubes have dissolved.

Pour the mixture into a collins glass. Express the lemon twists and discard. Place the glass in the freezer to settle for 2 to 3 minutes, until the froth tightens up at the top like a Guinness. Pull the glass from the freezer. Poke a hole into the foamy top with a straw, and then pour the soda water slowly into the hole as you see the cylindrical foam cap rise over the top of the glass.

NOTE • Bottled soda water gives better lift than home-carbonated. We pour the bottled soda into the used cocktail tin and then from there into the drink.

CORPSE REVIVER #2

Hailing from a long lineage of wake-up-call cocktails, this particular member of the corpse reviver family is the most famous and is often associated with the Harry Craddock–era American Bar at The Savoy in London (1920 to 1938). This association is no doubt due to Craddock's indelible characterizations of the drink in his authoritative *The Savoy Cocktail Book*: "To be taken before 11 a.m., or whenever steam and energy are needed," while also warning that "four of these taken in swift succession will quickly unrevive the corpse again." In this perfectly balanced drink, in which aromatic citrus and absinthe flavors provide the nasal tingle, all major ingredients are traditionally portioned in equal parts, with a single dash of absinthe. At Maison Premiere, we enjoy absinthe liberally and so increase the portion to a teaspoon, also adding a teaspoon of rich simple syrup to give some much-needed length and finish to the palate.

1 teaspoon Rich Simple Syrup (page 175)
1 teaspoon Duplais Verte absinthe
¾ ounce lemon juice
¾ ounce Mattei Cap Corse Quinquina Blanc vermouth
¾ ounce Combier orange liqueur
1 ounce Hayman's London Dry gin

In a Boston tin or cobbler shaker, combine the simple syrup, absinthe, lemon juice, vermouth, orange liqueur, and gin. Fill the shaker with ice, cover, and shake vigorously. Fine strain the mixture into a cocktail glass.

SAZERAC

Some say that the Sazerac is America's oldest and first cocktail, even predating the term cocktail. Others contend the Sazerac was originally a Cognac drink, which, due to the dearth of brandy from ruined European grape harvests of the 1860s and '70s, became a rye drink. Rye whiskey soon became the de facto national spirit, fueling the era of the Manhattan, Old Fashioned, and Sazerac alike.

Originally, a Sazerac preparation (or its cousin, the Old Fashioned) can be seen as a quick and simple treatment aimed at making harsh whiskeys (which would have been almost all of them) more palatable, but it swiftly became a part of New Orleans identity. From palaces like the Roosevelt Hotel to the dives of Bourbon Street, one can still find countless versions of the Sazerac.

Before Prohibition, absinthe was popular in its own right, though always hailing from Europe. But after the absinthe ban and Prohibition, several producers created local New Orleans absinthe recipes, with one of them, Herbsaint (a subtle near-anagram of *absinthe*), becoming the de facto pastis with which to rinse the Sazerac glass.

Tradition says that the Sazerac glass should be rinsed with absinthe and the spirit then dumped. To that end, bartenders would frequently toss a spinning dash-of-absinthe-containing glass many feet into the air to thoroughly coat its interior before deftly catching it, that classic bit of showmanship for which American bars are famous. (The Sazerac Bar in the Roosevelt New Orleans hotel is a good place to see this technique in action.) But since, at heart, we are an absinthe bar, we suggest not a drop be wasted. We conserve the absinthe selected for your Sazerac in a little sidecar glass and serve it in tandem with your cocktail.

¼ ounce absinthe
6 heavy dashes of Peychaud's bitters
6 heavy dashes of Creole bitters
1 teaspoon Demerara Simple Syrup (page 175)
2 ounces Wild Turkey 101 rye whiskey
Lemon twist, for garnish

At Maison we perform the two operations of this drink simultaneously, employing both hands at once. Feel free to make it sequential, of course.

Fill a room-temperature rocks glass with crushed ice. Add the absinthe over the crushed ice. Now, while that sits, in a mixing glass, combine the bitters, Demerara simple syrup, and whiskey, then fill with ice. With one hand, stir the mixing glass, while, with the other, swizzle or gently agitate the rocks glass until its sides are coated with absinthe. Strain the absinthe through a Hawthorne strainer into a little sidecar glass. Dump the crushed ice from the rocks glass, which is now absinthe coated and chilled. Strain the mixing-glass contents into the chilled rocks glass. Express a lemon twist over the drink, then discard.

IMPROVED HURRICANE

OBITUARY

After five or six years of being (mostly) on the menu, our reconstructed Hurricane, we decided, could use a bit of a makeover. Driving this impulse was massive expansion in the rum market. Since the opening of Maison Premiere, interest in the great variety of regional Caribbean rums had exploded, resulting in hundreds of new products hitting the market; in other words, myriad new flavors to paint into our cocktails. Chief among this new guard was a portfolio of products imported and/or created by Ed Hamilton (the self-proclaimed Minister of Rum and one of the world's great experts on the subject), including unctuous pot still rums from Jamaica that add depth, richness, umami, and delicious funk to our original, fruity drink. (Word to the wise: try working your way through each of Ed Hamilton's various rums in the Improved Hurricane, as each one offers a delightful new variation. The always-limited St. Lucian Pot Still is our favorite.)

1 ounce Passion Fruit Syrup (page 177)
1 ounce lemon juice
1 ounce Hamilton Pot Still Black rum
1 ounce Rhum J.M Blanc 100 proof
2 large straws, for garnish

In a hurricane glass, add the passion fruit syrup, lemon juice, and rums. Insert a swizzle stick and fill the glass with crushed ice over the swizzle stick. Agitate the mixture gently with the swizzle for about 15 seconds, then remove it carefully. Add more crushed ice over the top and garnish with two opposing large straws.

We adore this old New Orleans martini variation, the Obituary. Despite its morbid name—or perhaps because of it—the cocktail has been surprisingly beloved at Maison Premiere. Simply described, it is a classic gin martini with precisely 6 dashes of absinthe added. And while that small amount may not sound like much, it adds herbal complexity, complementing gin, vermouth, and lemon oil equally. That new dimension turns the stiff, familiar martini into a multilayered, ethereally aromatic gem. Be careful with the absinthe—a loose hand will result in a surfeit of this intense spirit, which can easily overpower the rest of the drink. Our version of this cocktail is adapted from a Lafitte's Blacksmith Shop Bar recipe, which first appeared in the book *New Orleans Drinks and How to Mix 'Em*, published in 1938.

6 dashes of absinthe
1 ounce Dolin dry vermouth
2¼ ounces Hayman's London Dry gin
Lemon twist, for garnish

In a mixing glass, add the absinthe, vermouth, and gin and fill with ice. Stir and strain the mixture into a chilled coupe. Express the lemon twist over the drink, then discard.

VIEUX CARRÉ

NEW ORLEANS BUCK

Easily one of New Orleans's most recognizable drinks, the Vieux Carré—a spicy, strong, and strapping celebration of brown spirits that originated at the Hotel Monteleone in the early 1930s— is also no stranger to the dimly lit craft-cocktail haunts of NYC. However, many bartenders outside the Big Easy tend to overly complicate the recipe, adding fancier whiskey, house-made bitters, and richer vermouth. After tasting the cocktail with all manner of additions, "improvements," and twists, we endorse the directness and classicism of a more humble rendering, using widely available bottlings and the classic combination of Angostura bitters and Peychaud's bitters. Also note: Bigger, bolder, brasher vermouth does not improve the drink. Stick with Cinzano or another lighter-style sweet vermouth.

1 dash of Angostura bitters
3 dashes of Peychaud's bitters
¼ ounce Bénédictine
1 ounce Wild Turkey 101 rye whiskey
1 ounce Dudognon VSOP Cognac
1 ounce Cinzano Rosso

In a mixing glass, combine the Angostura bitters, Peychaud's bitters, Bénédictine, rye, Cognac, and Cinzano, and fill with ice. Stir the mixture rapidly, adding ice as needed, and strain into a rocks glass over ice.

Though rum is often overshadowed by whiskey and Cognac in the annals of New Orleans drinking, it finds the spotlight in this namesake buck. A buck, of course, is a classic cocktail form that combines citrus and ginger beer (or ale) with a base spirit to create a vibrant and refreshing cocktail that buzzes with intensity from all the strong flavors. And while this buck might have a kinship to the well-known Dark 'n' Stormy, it can be diversely interpreted by the many shades of rum now available to the intrepid drink mixer. Once again, we quite prefer Ed Hamilton's imports.

¾ ounce lime juice
¾ ounce Ginger Syrup (page 175)
2 ounces Hamilton Pot Still Black rum
Ginger ale, to taste
Mint bouquet, Angostura bitters,
    1 large straw, for garnish

In a Boston tin shaker, combine the lime juice, ginger syrup, and rum. Fill the shaker with ice, cover, and shake vigorously. Strain the mixture into an ice-filled collins glass. Top with ginger ale. Garnish with a mint bouquet, a few drops of Angostura bitters, and the large straw.

Garden Cocktails

❧

In the early and formative years of Maison Premiere, much energy was given to building a julep section for the menu, paying tribute to the Southern drinking culture that so inspired us. We call these and other summery daytime drinks "garden cocktails," though they may certainly be enjoyed on warm nights, post gloaming.

PIMM'S CUP

Bright and summery and floridly garnished, the Pimm's Cup is based on and named for Pimm's No. 1 Cup, a gin-based health tonic with a secret recipe invented in the 1840s by James Pimm, who was, coincidentally, a London oyster bar owner. One hundred years later at New Orleans's Napoleon House, the Pimm's Cup cocktail was invented, meant to provide a refreshing, low-alcohol drink that patrons could enjoy in multiples during the midsummer swelter of the French Quarter. Back in England, the cocktail became the signature drink of Wimbledon, where a Pimm's bar was established in 1971. Almost since opening, Maison Premiere has offered a seasonal Pimm's Cup variation (totaling about forty-two), but it wasn't until the summer of 2022 that we added our version of the original to the menu in all its flowery glory.

2 dashes of Angostura bitters
2 dashes of orange bitters
3 drops of orange flower water
⅛ teaspoon saline (1 vial)
-¼ ounce Ginger Syrup (page 175)
¾ ounce lemon juice
½ ounce Lemon Cordial (page 177)
2 thin slices of cucumber
1 ounce Pimm's No. 1
1 ounce Hayman's London Dry gin
Ginger beer, to top
Mint sprigs, borage flowers, lemon zest grated on a
    Microplane, and cucumber ribbons, for garnish

Combine the two bitters, orange flower water, saline, ginger syrup, lemon juice, lemon cordial, cucumber slices, Pimm's, and gin in a Boston tin shaker. Fill the shaker with ice, cover, and shake vigorously. Strain into a collins glass filled with hand-cracked ice cubes. Add a splash of ginger beer (1½ to 2 ounces). Garnish with mint sprigs, borage flowers, and grated lemon zest, and place a skewer of cucumber ribbons over the top of the glass. Finally, add a straw and serve.

MAISON BLOODY MARY

In the process of designing the Maison Bloody Mary, we knew we couldn't be parsimonious with flavor. It had to have impact. We created a standardized base puree to enhance the drink's overall depth and texture, by including celery, onion, carrot, garlic, and chipotle peppers, in addition to the tomato juice. For spice and savory notes, we combined several classic ingredients with some original additions: Worcestershire sauce, Dijon mustard, horseradish, and Tabasco sauce. But perhaps the real secret is the addition of a half ounce of our very own Maison Premiere Oyster Stout, a traditional stout style brewed with the shells of oysters, giving a lactic hit of mineral salinity. It's a wonderfully complex stew of flavors, and feel free to use any good oyster stout you can find.

3 hard dashes of Tabasco sauce
Freshly ground black pepper, to taste
½ ounce lemon juice
½ ounce oyster stout
1½ ounces vodka
5 ounces bloody Mary mix (recipe follows)
Tall celery stalk with leaves, lemon wedge, skewered pickled vegetable
    selection (e.g., cauliflower, purple onion, turnip, and a caper berry
    and olive stuffed with sea beans), toddy straw, for garnish

In a poco grande glass, combine the Tabasco, black pepper, lemon juice, oyster stout, and vodka, and stir with 3 ice cubes. Then add the bloody Mary mix and stir to combine. Garnish with a tall celery stalk and one lemon wedge. Then, skewer three pickled vegetables and insert into the glass. Finish with a little more freshly ground black pepper on top and a toddy straw.

MAISON BLOODY MARY MIX

3 celery stalks
1 white onion, peeled
1 large carrot, peeled
3 garlic cloves
36 ounces tomato juice
6 canned chipotle peppers
1 cup prepared horseradish
1 cup Dijon mustard
8 ounces Worcestershire sauce
1 tablespoon salt
½ tablespoon black pepper
3 ounces Tabasco sauce

Juice the celery, onion, carrot, and garlic, and combine their liquids with the tomato juice in a large bucket. Blend the chipotle peppers with the horseradish, mustard, and a little of the tomato juice mixture. Add the blended chipotle pepper mixture, Worcestershire sauce, salt, pepper, and Tabasco to the large bucket of vegetable juice, stir well, and refrigerate overnight.

MAKES ENOUGH FOR 10 MAISON BLOODY MARYS

VARIATION: MAISON BLOODY CAESAR

This is quite similar to our bloody Mary but adds a half ounce of clam brine into the mix. It is an elaborately garnished affair as well—"plated" on an iced saucer with a briny oyster.

IN THE MAQUIS

A study in green, this cocktail was inspired by head bartender Will Elliott's trip to the historic Chartreuse distillery in the mountains of eastern France, where the monks tell stories of locals eluding Nazi patrols while hiding in the brambly woods, for which the French word is *maquis*. Like Chartreuse, the drink is very herbal, vegetal, and verdant. A take on Malört, the bitter Schnapps-like spirit heavily consumed in Chicago, Bësk is a sort of milder, less bitter version of European alpine herbal liqueur and is made by the American distiller Letherbee. Of course, we had to get that authentic alpine note in there anyway via the gentian-flavored genepy. All of the above interact gorgeously with one of our favorite gins, whose production dates back to the seventeenth century on the island of Menorca, Spain, where it was created to sate the thirst of visiting British sailors.

3 dashes of celery bitters
¼ ounce Letherbee Bësk
+¼ ounce green Chartreuse
½ ounce Lemon Cordial (page 177)
¾ ounce lemon juice
1 ounce Herbetet genepy
1 ounce Xoriguer Mahón gin
4 inch-long pieces of celery
Interior celery leaves, pink peppercorns, lime zest,
    1 large straw, for garnish

In a Boston tin shaker, combine the bitters, Bësk, Chartreuse, lemon cordial, lemon juice, genepy, and gin, and add the celery to the shaker. Fill with ice and shake with a short but vigorous shake. Strain the mixture into a stemmed beer or white wine glass. Garnish with a few interior celery leaves, some pink peppercorns, and thin threads of lime zest. Add the straw.

MINT JULEP

The great classic of bourbon country and the South, proper mint juleps became attractive for us at Maison only when the specialty equipment supplier Cocktail Kingdom began manufacturing metal julep tins, essential in amplifying the chill of the drink. While our preparation is quite traditional, it's very much informed by New Orleans bartending legend Chris McMillian, whose instructional and historical YouTube videos are gems of cocktail erudition. Indeed, one particular video, which includes the recitation of a julep poem, is required viewing for every Maison bartender. We take to heart his exhortation to be gentle with the mint leaves and merely give them a gentle slap and a rub on the interior of the cup before discarding them. Mint will reappear as a small bouquet into which the straw is tucked, as every sip of julep should be accompanied by a strong whiff of mint perfume. We chose to use hand-cracked ice cubes in our juleps instead of the standard crushed ice because it fits with the rusticity we perceive in this drink. To us, crushed ice in this setting seems a little overly manicured, even though it's the status quo for bars around the country.

The word *julep*, as we understand it, comes from an ancient Arabic word referring to anything that's aromatic. How it came over from Africa and the Arabian Peninsula and became a cocktail, we don't know, though it's been postulated to have originated as a *genever* drink, meaning that the julep wasn't the sole possession of the South. While the definition of the genre is vague—something about a spirit being served over crushed ice, often with mint—we've taken it as a crushed-ice cocktail served in a julep tin. With that in mind, we see the julep as a genre and have riffed on it prolifically over the years.

3–4 fresh mint leaves
1 dash of Angostura bitters
¼ ounce Demerara Simple Syrup (page 175)
2 ounces Four Roses bourbon
Generous bouquet of fresh mint, 2 short straws,
    for garnish

Hand crack a cup of ice by your own method (we use a mallet and a Lewis bag). Clap the mint leaves in your hands to release the oils, place them inside a julep tin and rub them around the interior to coat all the surfaces, then discard. To the tin, add the bitters, simple syrup, and bourbon, and fill with hand-cracked ice cubes until it's half-full. Give a quick stir and then add more hand-cracked cubes until they are mounded over the top. Garnish with an extravagant mint bouquet with the straws tucked in, almost hidden among the mint leaves.

AGUA BENTA JULEP

DE SURCO SLING

In 2013, juleps were our most notable and growing cocktail category, and so we began to expand our house style to go beyond bourbon and mint to involve more and more spirits and flavors not necessarily associated with the julep. This was also our first cachaça cocktail (cachaça being the Brazilian cousin to rhum agricole, involving the distillation of raw sugarcane juice rather than molasses; most rum in the world is molasses based, or what the French would call rhum industriel). The agua benta was an early example of this branching out; it exchanged whiskey for cachaça and was augmented with the vegetal funk of celery, the fruity heat of the Peruvian ají chile, and the herbal kick of the famous French gentian aperitif Suze. The result was a dangerously drinkable mix, akin to a lightly spiced daiquiri.

1 teaspoon Suze gentian liqueur
+¼ ounce Lime Cordial (page 177)
–½ ounce Maison 7-Spice Chai Syrup (page 176)
½ ounce lemon juice
½ ounce celery juice
1¾ ounces Avuá cachaça
Lime zest grated on a Microplane, ají chile, 2 small green paper straws, for garnish

In a julep tin, combine the Suze, lime cordial, spice syrup, lemon juice, celery juice, and cachaça, and fill with hand-cracked ice cubes until it's half-full. Give a quick stir and then add more hand-cracked cubes until they are mounded over the top. Garnish with the grated lime zest, the ají chile, and two straws.

This soft summer sling (a sling is simply spirit plus water, sweetened and flavored) is primed for the season. Capurro is a soft, semifloral Peruvian pisco, and it perfectly frames the subtleties of strawberry and parsley. Likely the only lesser-known ingredient in this cocktail, Amaro dell'Erborista is a very natural and traditional amaro by Varnelli distillery, sporting a bracingly bitter spine that's rounded and complemented by notes of rhubarb, gentian, and even sandalwood.

1 teaspoon Amaro dell'Erborista
¼ ounce Rich Simple Syrup (page 175)
¼ ounce Giffard crème de fraise (strawberry liqueur)
½ ounce lemon juice
½ ounce Lemon Cordial (page 177)
1¾ ounces parsley-infused Capurro pisco (see Note)
4 strawberries, 2 left whole and 2 sliced
Parsley sprig, for garnish

To a Boston tin shaker, add all the liquid ingredients and 2 whole strawberries. Fill the shaker with ice cubes and shake vigorously but briefly. (To keep them concentrated, drinks served over crushed ice don't get long shakes since crushed ice melts quickly.) Fine strain into a collins glass, then fill the glass with crushed ice, mounded over the top. Tuck the sliced strawberries into the side of the glass near the rim. Finish with a sprig of parsley.

NOTE • Parsley infuses spirits quickly and powerfully, so to infuse it into pisco, add one bunch to a bottle of pisco and allow to sit for 20 minutes at room temperature before removing the parsley. Strain if necessary.

HOUSE OF WINDSOR

VANDERBILT HOLIDAY

This elegant ode to summer and citrus is a quite ideal embodiment of what we imagine a "garden cocktail" to be. The use of two wines makes it less potent in alcohol—an important summertime element, given the common desire to extend the cool, refreshing experience of garden drinking without getting sloshed—while the lemon provides lift and the gin and bitters bestow body and complexity. Hence a dreamy daytime drink is dreamed.

> 1 dash of celery bitters
> ½ ounce lemon juice
> ¾ ounce Lemon Cordial (page 177)
> ¾ ounce Pineau de Charentes
> ¾ ounce grapefruit Riesling
> 1 ounce Ransom Old Tom gin
> Chopped dill, lemon zest grated on a
>   Microplane, 2 lemon rounds, 1 large
>   straw, for garnish

To a Boston tin shaker, add the bitters, lemon juice, lemon cordial, Pineau de Charentes, Riesling, and gin. Fill the shaker with ice, cover, and shake vigorously. Strain into a collins glass filled with hand-cracked ice cubes. Garnish with chopped dill and grated lemon zest, and tuck the lemon rounds into the drink against the wall of the glass. Insert the straw.

Raspberries are lovely and so is Chartreuse. So why not try them together in a union consummated by lemon juice and frothed with egg white? All in all, this unabashed reimagining of the classic Clover Club cocktail is perfectly suited as a midafternoon-in-the-garden delight.

> ½ ounce green Chartreuse herbal
>   liqueur
> ¾ ounce lemon juice
> ¾ ounce Raspberry Syrup (page 175)
> 1 ounce framboise eau-de-vie
> 1 egg white
> 1 raspberry
> Angostura bitters, to taste
> Skewered raspberry, for garnish

In a Boston tin shaker, combine the Chartreuse, lemon juice, raspberry syrup, eau-de-vie, egg white, and raspberry. Dry shake. Add ice and then shake again. Strain the mixture into a stemmed sour glass or coupe. Add a few drops of Angostura bitters and use a toothpick to create bitters art by spreading the bitters into linear designs in the frothy foam (as suggested in the photo for the Whiskeytown Regatta, page 149). Top with a skewered raspberry.

ROSETTI

A treatise on summer berries and all things deep crimson, the Rosetti is a juicy julep, racy and quenching. Crème de cassis, a sweet liqueur made from black currants, is native to Dijon, France, whence comes the famed mustard. Fruit and mustard are often combined there, and when drinking good cassis, one is often left with a hint of spice in the finish. Combining the puckering acidity of sloe berry and lemon and the herbal complexity of Cocchi's Rosa vermouth, this julep nearly defies the genre in its supple and lightening elegance.

¾ ounce Hayman's sloe gin
¾ ounce Giffard crème de cassis
1 ounce lemon juice
1 ounce Cocchi Rosa vermouth
Generous bouquet of fresh mint, 2 short straws,
  rosebuds, 3 drops rose flower water

To a julep tin, combine the gin, crème de cassis, lemon juice, and vermouth, and fill with crushed ice until it's half-full. Give a quick stir and then add more crushed ice until it's mounded over the top. Garnish with an extravagant mint bouquet with the straws tucked in, almost hidden among the mint leaves. Nest the rosebuds in the mint, then with an eyedropper add a few drops of rose flower water onto the rosebuds.

MAISON SHERRY COBBLER

Sometimes called the Cosmo of the 1860s, the sherry cobbler was the cocktail of its time. Instrumental—along with the julep—in the invention of the straw (because it was almost impossible to consume the second half of these highly garnished crushed-iced drinks without tipping the cup and having its contents fall on your face), it was also the first cocktail as popular with women as it was with men, according to one bartending manual of its time. It's also quite low in alcohol, and therefore it can be drunk in some quantity—always a plus. Our technique of using four separate styles of sherry confers complexity and dimension well beyond the original simplicity of the drink and is unique in the cocktail world, to our knowledge. As it was back in the nineteenth century, the garnish must be extravagant and garish; if you are wondering if you have heaped enough vegetation on top of the sherry cobbler you are about to serve, you probably haven't.

1 teaspoon allspice dram
¼ ounce Demerara Simple Syrup (page 175)
½ ounce lemon juice
½ ounce pineapple juice
¾ ounce blueberry or blackberry jam
¾ ounce amontillado sherry
¾ ounce Manzanilla sherry
¾ ounce oloroso sherry
¾ ounce Pedro Ximénez sherry
The kitchen sink (e.g., 2 halved blackberries,
   1 thinly sliced half-moon orange, mint bouquet,
   1 toddy straw), for garnish

In a Boston tin shaker, combine the dram, simple syrup, lemon juice, pineapple juice, blueberry jam, and sherries. Fill with crushed ice and perform the one-handed whip shake until the drink is well cooled. Dump the mixture into a poco grande glass. Garnish gaudily with the blackberries, orange, mint bouquet, and straw. (See photo for garnish.)

THE SHINING PATH

This bracing aperitif is the perfect segue into a fantastic dinner or a first drink of the afternoon. Though brightened by the lively citrus of lemon cordial and the delicate sophistication of elderflower, it has a boldly bitter backbone that keeps one thirsty for more. Two of our favorite European herbal liqueurs, Salers and Avèze, offer that pleasing vegetal bitterness that only gentian can provide, and in our opinion, always taste best in the daytime!

½ ounce lemon juice
½ ounce Lemon Cordial (page 177)
½ ounce St-Germain elderflower liqueur
½ ounce Avèze
¾ ounce Salers
Float of Granada-Vallett pomegranate amaro
3–4 safflower blossoms, lemon zest, toddy straw,
    for garnish

In a stemmed pilsner glass, add the lemon juice, lemon cordial, St-Germain, Avèze, and Salers. Fill the glass with crushed ice and give it a little swizzle. Mound more crushed ice over the top. For the garnish, first, insert a long paper straw. Then add the float of pomegranate amaro, garnish with the safflower blossoms, and finish with lemon zest.

VIVA ALBERTI

Strega, *both the Italian word for "witch" as well as a saffron-infused Italian liqueur, became* an object of fascination at Maison Premiere around 2011 because of its uniquely minty and anise-inflected flavor. Strega's creation in 1860 is owed to a father-and-son team with the surname Alberti, hence the name of the cocktail. A joyful, refreshing contortion of a French 75—refreshing yet rich, with herbal top notes—this drink could also be called a Strega spritz, fortified with Cognac and topped with cava. In creating this, we hoped to subvert the ubiquitous Aperol spritz, which, to us, while delicious, seems more like a soda than a cocktail.

3 dashes of Angostura orange bitters
1 teaspoon Cappelletti Amaro
½ ounce lemon juice
½ ounce Dudognon Reserve Cognac
1 ounce Strega
1 ounce cava
Double-feathered orange twist (see Note), pink
    peppercorns, 2 straws, for garnish

In a small wineglass, add the bitters, amaro, lemon juice, Cognac, and Strega, and fill with hand-cracked ice cubes. Top with cava. Then place a double-feathered orange twist on top and sprinkle with pink peppercorns. Serve with the straws.

NOTE • To create a double-feathered twist, use a peeler to cut a wide twist from the orange. Trim its ends with a paring knife, then carefully make several parallel incisions on each end of the twist to simulate feathers.

GOLDEN CUP

A true garden cocktail if there ever was one, the Golden Cup was created to echo in flavor and sensation the inspiring tenderness of a late spring garden, alive with young flowers, *fraise du bois*, and fresh herbs. Hence, rose and strawberry flavors are burnished by the citrus and spice in Pimm's and buttressed by lemon juice. The other inspiration for this drink is the gin from Neversink Spirits, a wonderful craft distillery in New York, which specializes in apples. As such, the gin integrates apple-friendly botanicals (cinnamon, cardamom, star anise) and a base spirit made from apples. A new member of the julep family, this drink is meant to be sipped in dappled sunlight outdoors and is served in one of our golden julep tins (feel free to use any color, though) to promote maximum optimism.

  ¼ teaspoon rose flower water

  ½ ounce lemon juice

  ½ ounce Giffard crème de fraise (strawberry liqueur)

  1 ounce Pimm's No. 1

  1 ounce Neversink gin

  1 strawberry, thinly sliced into a fan, mint sprig, fresh
      borage flowers, 2 small straws, for garnish

In a julep tin, combine the rose flower water, lemon juice, crème de fraise, Pimm's, and gin. Place a swizzle stick in the tin, then add a scoop of crushed ice. Agitate the liquids with the ice until they are combined and slushy. Gently remove the swizzle stick. Top the tin with crushed ice in a big, generous mound. Garnish with a fanned strawberry, mint sprig, fresh borage flowers, and the straws.

BARBER OF SEVILLE

As much inspired by the scents wafting from an Italian pasticceria as by any cocktail bar or front-porch julep (a spirit-and-water-based cocktail served over crushed ice), the Barber of Seville is an inversion of typical julep-derived proportions. Simply stated, rather than garnishing whiskey with some modifier liquors or cordials, this recipe employs rye whiskey as the modifier and lightly bitters it with Cappelletti Amaro. A liberal full ounce of Manzanilla sherry adds the funk and a subtle hook of salinity, while orange flower water brightens the whole mix. Combined with a finely grated candied Marcona almond and orange zest, it reminds one of walking into an Italian bakery in the morning, replete with marzipan, baking spice, and orange zest. A truly Mediterranean julep.

3 dashes of orange bitters
½ ounce orange flower water
½ ounce lemon juice
+¼ ounce Maison Orgeat (page 176)
½ ounce Old Overholt rye whiskey
¾ ounce Cappelletti Amaro
1 ounce Hidalgo Manzanilla sherry
Toasted Marcona almond grated on a Microplane,
    orange zest, paper parasol, 2 sip-stick straws,
    for garnish

In a julep tin, combine the bitters, orange flower water, lemon juice, orgeat, whiskey, amaro, and sherry. Top with crushed ice, swizzle, remove the swizzle stick, then mound crushed ice over the top. To garnish, insert a blown-back paper parasol, sprinkle the grated almond over the top, add some threads of fine orange zest, and insert the straws.

Drawing Room Drinks

✤

These are the kind of cocktails you could imagine sipping cozily in a den while reclining in an armchair—rich, powerful, comforting, and burnished drinks that incite reflection and rumination. While they are perfect for a late afternoon, going on evening, some are also a tad sweet, making them ideal substitutions for dessert and a terrific accompaniment to an engrossing book after dinner.

ADONIS

We unearthed this one while researching classic drinks that employed sherry, which was com- ing back into fashion as a cocktail ingredient during our early years. Named for what may have been, in 1884, the very first Broadway musical, the Adonis features no shortage of assertive ingredients, making for a low-ABV drink of high impact, notably with the nutty and buttery stamp of sherry. Maison's version honors Broadway in its performative aspect: To garnish, one must use a channel knife to carve an exceedingly long single twist out of an orange and then tie that twist into an old sailor's knot, the figure eight.

> 3 dashes of Angostura orange bitters
> ¾ ounce Pedro Ximénez sherry
> 1 ounce oloroso sherry
> 1½ ounces Cocchi Torino vermouth
> 1 orange zested into an exceedingly long twist,
>   for garnish

In a mixing glass, combine the bitters, sherries, and vermouth. Fill the glass with ice, stir, and strain into an Adonis glass filled with ice cubes. Cut a very, very long orange twist—at least 18 inches—with a channel knife and tie it into a classic figure-eight knot.

OLD FASHIONED

As classic as it gets, the Maison Old Fashioned bows to the primitive simplicity of the original—which was quite obviously a way to enhance and make more palatable the undoubtedly rough, coarse spirits of the day—but shows further respect by making it with elevated, elegant technique. First, we always ask what spirit the guest wants, as it's not always rye (many choose brandy). The double orange and lemon twist both highlight and offset the spirits.

3 dashes of Angostura orange bitters
3 dashes of Angostura bitters
¼ ounce Demerara Simple Syrup (page 175)
1 ounce Ragtime rye
1 ounce Wild Turkey 101 rye whiskey
Orange twist, lemon twist, for garnish

In a room-temperature rocks glass, combine both bitters and the simple syrup, and stir together. Then add the rye and rye whiskey, followed by ice cubes, which are stirred in the glass until they begin to melt and precipitate condensation on the outer rim. Continuing the stir (as described on page 64), tong in a couple more cubes until they melt enough to become submerged in the liquid. Express an orange and lemon twist over the drink, then insert them into the glass.

MP CHANCELLOR COCKTAIL

FUTURE DAYS

A handful of stirred cocktails benefit from being premixed and stored indefinitely in the freezer. Many people do this with so-called freezer martinis. This classic—a Manhattan variation using scotch (with our addition of cinnamon syrup)—is such a drink. When it emerges from the cold, it provides an introductory pleasure before its actual consumption, as the guest observes the languorous viscosity of the drink oozing into the glass. We prebatch the drink, stir it to perfection, then bottle it in a crystal decanter, which is kept in the freezer. When a guest orders one, we pour it tableside into a frozen martini glass.

> 3 dashes of orange bitters
> 1 teaspoon cinnamon syrup
> ¾ ounce Mauro Vergano Bianco
>   vermouth
> ¾ ounce tawny port
> 2 ounces blended scotch
> Orange twist, for garnish

As mentioned above, Maison prebatches this drink, but here are the instructions for making a one-off: Chill a martini glass. In a mixing glass, combine the bitters, cinnamon syrup, vermouth, tawny port, and scotch, and fill with ice. Stir the mixture and strain into a chilled V-shaped martini glass. Express the orange twist over the drink, then discard.

An eclectic blend of spirits almost experimental in their combination, this drink was aptly inspired by the 1973 album of the same name by the progressive German band Can. On paper, this cacophony appears like it won't work, but nevertheless it does, delighting the tongue while also confounding it. One note: Most Maison drinks can be fairly replicated by replacing one or more brands with comparable substitutes. This is not one of them. Without these specific brands, it refuses to coalesce.

> 3 dashes of grapefruit bitters
> 5 dashes of absinthe
> +¼ ounce Demerara Simple Syrup
>   (page 175)
> 1 ounce Luxardo Amaro Abano
> 1 ounce Ransom's Old Tom gin
> 1 ounce Banhez mezcal
> Grapefruit twist, for garnish

In a mixing glass, combine the bitters, absinthe, simple syrup, amaro, gin, and mezcal, and fill with ice. Stir the mixture and strain into a chilled coupe. Garnish with a grapefruit twist.

WHARFHOUSE

ROUND ROBIN

The worldly, intriguing man who inspired this drink lived on North Haven Island, Maine, in a large seaside house whose facade resembled the prow of a tall ship. This nutty, spiced, stirred drink is meant to warm from the inside out, as one might desire while facing the sea from a second-floor drawing room on a cold, foggy Maine day.

> 3 drops of orange flower water
> 3 dashes of Angostura bitters
> 3 dashes of Angostura orange bitters
> ¾ ounce Pedro Ximénez sherry
> ¾ ounce Michelberger Mountain
>   herbal liqueur
> ¾ ounce Armagnac Castarède
> ¾ ounce Santa Teresa rum
> Orange twist, for garnish

In a mixing glass, combine the orange flower water, bitters, sherry, Michelberger Mountain, Armagnac, and rum, and fill with ice. Stir the mixture and strain into a chilled Nick & Nora glass. Express an orange twist over the drink, then discard.

Another example of Maison's (never- ending?) alpine-spirits and amaro obsession, this one comes down out of the Alps and into the Rhône valley to pick up an ounce of Beaujolais wine, which froths into a foamy head upon shaking, giving the drink incredible body. Once, the producer of the wine we were using for this, a young Frenchman, happened to anonymously come into the bar and saw his precious creation disappearing into a mixing tin. His mouth gaped in surprise but then turned to a smile after his first sip.

> ½ ounce Braulio amaro
> +½ ounce Maison Grenadine
>   (page 177)
> ¾ ounce lemon juice
> 1 ounce Beaujolais wine
> 1 ounce genepy

To a Boston tin or cobbler shaker, add the amaro, grenadine, lemon juice, wine, and genepy. Fill the shaker with ice, cover, and shake vigorously. Fine strain the mixture into a chilled, stemmed sour glass.

LADY LYNDON

Warm cocktails are hardly in fashion, but like the toddy, they have their place. Don't overlook this one in the fall and winter months. Lemon juice, raspberry syrup, absinthe, and various fortified wines come together to form a potently aromatic and intense base that welcomes warm water and the touch of rose-infused cream. The daintier the tea set this is served in, the better. The accompanying madeleine is, of course, optional.

¼ ounce Germain-Robin absinthe
+¼ ounce Raspberry Syrup (page 175)
½ ounce Pineau des Charentes
½ ounce Mauro Vergano Americano
¾ ounce lemon juice
¾ ounce framboise eau-de-vie
Hot water
Rose cream (recipe follows), confectioners' sugar, mint
   sprig, 3 raspberries, for garnish

In the smaller half of a Boston tin shaker, combine the absinthe, raspberry syrup, Pineau des Charentes, Mauro Vergano Americano, lemon juice, and eau-de-vie. Fill the larger tin halfway with scalding hot water. Sink the tin containing the spirits into the hot water. (If the hot water is at the right level, the top tin will almost completely submerge.) Cover with a coaster and let the cocktail warm for a few minutes. In the meantime, warm a teacup with hot water and ready its saucer. When the cup is warm, dump the hot water and pour in the cocktail. Top with hot water. Then spoon rose cream over the top. Sprinkle a little confectioners' sugar on it and add a tiny mint sprig. On the saucer include a skewer with the raspberries.

NOTE • Rose cream: In a Boston tin shaker, combine 2 ounces heavy whipping cream, ¾ teaspoon Demerara sugar, and ¼ ounce rose flower water. Shake until you get stiff peaks.

LIGHT GREEN FELLOW

A heady dessert drink can reveal our innermost selves: We malign it for being intolerably unctuous while licking the too-soon-empty glass. This one is unassailable as it forces you into the same bed with such combative personalities as Cognac, coffee liqueur, crème de menthe, amaro, and almond-cherry grappa. It's the cream, that usually laughable cocktail ingredient, to which we owe our deepest gratitude for keeping the peace.

¾ ounce heavy cream
¼ ounce Dudognon Cognac
¼ ounce caffè moka liqueur
¼ ounce Giffard Menthe-Pastille
¾ ounce Amaro Montenegro
¾ ounce Bortolo Nardini Mandorla grappa
Toasted Sicilian pistachio grated on a Microplane,
   for garnish

To a Boston tin or cobbler shaker, add the heavy cream, Cognac, caffè moka, Giffard Menthe-Pastille, amaro, and grappa. Fill the shaker with ice, cover, and shake vigorously. Fine strain the mixture into a Nick & Nora glass. Garnish with the grated pistachio.

WHISKEYTOWN REGATTA

Based on an old cocktail called the sixpenny crank, which employs both beer and gin, this was meant to be the cocktail home for our famous oyster stout. The beer's coffee notes seemed to call for a whiskey back, hence the addition of bourbon, which itself led to a craving for the honeyed scotch flavor of Drambuie, which ultimately brought us back to the espresso flavor of the stout. Dashes of absinthe, as always, pep things up and provide aromatic lift, as does the artistic garnishing license provided by the foam in a beer cocktail.

> 4 dashes of absinthe
> 1 teaspoon crème de cacao
> +¼ ounce caffè moka liqueur
> ¾ ounce lemon juice
> ¾ ounce Drambuie
> ¾ ounce Four Roses bourbon
> 1¼ ounces oyster stout
> Spray of absinthe (from spray bottle), bitters,
>   for garnish

To a Boston tin or cobbler shaker, add the absinthe, crème de cacao, caffè moka, lemon juice, Drambuie, bourbon, and stout. Fill the shaker with ice, cover, and shake vigorously. Strain into a chilled coupe. Spray the top with a bit of absinthe. To finish garnishing this drink perfectly, it helps to have bitters in a dasher bottle (a dash is considered to be 7 to 8 drops), which allows you to deposit the bitters in a straight line atop the foam, using a quick, precise swiping motion (see photograph on page 266). Use a toothpick to connect each bitters drop into a straight line, which can then be distorted into "tiger stripes."

Bracing and Urbane

This group of stiff, spirituous drinks falls into the genetic family of the martini. And why not? Such drinks require no time or place, no reason or mood. They are essential and universal, and we love them for their purity and their focused, keen-edged flavors. Diaphanous and often transparent in color, their crystalline clarity suggests action, lucidity, and presence of mind, while inducing the opposite—an irony in which we should all rejoice.

THE MARTINI

When people at the bar ask for a description of our standard martini? We don't have one, as this is one of the most personal preparations in existence. Do you prefer it drier or wetter? Gin or vodka? We assume gin but always ask. What kind of gin? Hayman's is our standard, but we have three kinds in the well—London Dry, Old Tom, and navy strength. We will shake a martini if asked to, though we don't recommend it. When it comes to martinis, we have no rules, but we do have opinions.

One unasked question is whether the guest prefers an olive or a twist because every martini at Maison Premiere is served with both—neatly presented atop a little sidecar of ice. Likewise, every martini, unless requested without, is finished with a lemon twist, which then is placed on the sidecar.

While the representative Maison Premiere cocktail is inventive and idiosyncratic, the martini—which would never be described so—is taken very seriously here, in part because of the importance of our raw bar, as the pleasure of swallowing a raw oyster is exponentially heightened when chased by a sip of martini.

When it comes to martinis, service protocol is paramount—whether you're making one at home for yourself or behind a bar for others. Something about the drink calls for ritual and respect. First, prepare your garnish. An ice-cold martini should never be kept waiting while its maker fiddles with accoutrements. So, on a little cutting board, trim the lemon twist and skewer the olives (we do so meticulously, serving always three olives). Now fetch a chilled martini glass. When we opened we used then-fashionable coupes, but around 2014 we became early re-adopters of the classic V-shaped martini glass.

In 2011, two-to-one (gin to vermouth) martinis were de rigueur. Then thanks to New York's Pegu Club and Audrey Saunders, along came the fifty-fifty, which never floated our boat. Today, our standard is two-and-a-quarter-to-one, and the big leap to "dry" is twelve-to-one.

The greatest problem with martinis is that they're never (and can never be) cold enough. The most effective method of chilling is to shake, but that utterly alters the drink's texture by adding aeration and ice crystals. The challenge becomes mathematical: the drink must be stirred quickly enough to achieve maximal chill while avoiding overdilution. You have a small window of time to get it cold enough. This requires a very rapid stir indeed and is the world's greatest reason for practicing that skill. As described on page 64, our technique at Maison involves adding ice while maintaining a high-rpm stir.

How do you know when it's been stirred enough? Practice, repetition, confidence, faith. An almost spiritual act, stirring a martini should be done with a Zen-like emptiness, filled only at the conclusion by the knowledge that you have tasted or can hold in your mind's eye the perfect martini, and that it has been equaled in this moment. Right now.

Olives, lemon twist, for garnish
3 dashes of Angostura orange bitters
1 ounce Dolin dry vermouth
2¼ ounces Hayman's London Dry gin

Prepare your mise en place first—skewer the olives and cut the twist and have a chilled glass ready—because you don't want to waste a second between preparing the drink and pouring it into the glass. In a mixing glass, combine the bitters, vermouth, and gin. Fill the glass with ice. Continue adding ice as you stir until all the secondary ice has been submerged. Strain the mixture into the chilled martini glass. Express the lemon twist with one hand over the stream as you're pouring the drink. Then place the lemon twist alongside three skewered olives on the sidecar.

GIBSON

We positively associate the Gibson with a steakhouse dinner, as a superior choice to a dirty martini and a truly wonderful option with oysters. The only difference from the martini is that it's served with cocktail onions on a skewer, not olives. Follow the Martini recipe above and swap the garnish.

TUXEDO #2

ALASKA

Of all the tuxedo cocktail variations (upward of 4), the number 2 from the Savoy book is the best. It's a classic martini variation with a little added herbaceousness and nuttiness for complexity and richness. The goal is to manage the potentially cloying marzipan presence of maraschino (a cherry pit liqueur). This endeavor is greatly aided by the existence of two great maraschinos, Vergnano and Bordiga, both of which are far more refined than the ubiquitous Luxardo version. The drink is a later variation on a cocktail invented at the Tuxedo Club in the 1890s, where the jacket of the same name also originated. This recipe is adapted from The Savoy Cocktail Book by Harry Craddock, originally published in 1930.

3 dashes of Angostura orange bitters
1 teaspoon Duplais Verte absinthe
½ ounce Vergnano or Bordiga
   maraschino liqueur
¾ ounce Dolin dry vermouth
1¾ ounces Hayman's London Dry gin
Lemon twist, for garnish

In a mixing glass, combine the bitters, absinthe, maraschino liqueur, vermouth, and gin, and fill with ice. Stir the mixture and strain into a chilled coupe. Express the lemon twist over the drink, then discard.

We always keep our eyes out for martini alternatives—drinks of the same genre and state of mind. This unusual classic marries gin with yellow Chartreuse. While the original called for Old Tom gin, we prefer the sharpness of London Dry. This recipe, like Tuxedo #2, is adapted from Harry Craddock's The Savoy Cocktail Book.

3 dashes of Angostura orange bitters
¾ ounce yellow Chartreuse
2½ ounces Hayman's navy strength gin
Lemon twist, for garnish

In a mixing glass, combine the bitters, Chartreuse, and gin, and fill with ice. Stir the mixture and strain into a chilled coupe. Express the lemon twist over the drink, then discard.

MP ARSENIC AND OLD LACE

Cocktail scholarship shows that this interesting drink began its life as "The Attention" in 1917, was renamed "the Atty" by Harry Craddock in 1930, and then was recast in 1941 under this name after the Broadway play and subsequent Cary Grant film. To our palate, crème de violette is one step from blue curaçao—that is, cloying and somewhat nauseating. So, how to make it work in a cocktail? We actively try to erase or at least push back on violette's cloyingness by ratcheting up the intensity of the accompanying spirits. Thus: La Muse Verte is an aggressive absinthe, the gin is navy strength (high proof), and Tempus Fugit is the most subtle of violette brands. Two twists are deployed, with the lemon's sharpness undercutting the orange. One might ask, why violette in the first place? Well, that's the cocktail. We can only assume the violette represents "old lace," while absinthe is "arsenic." This cocktail first appeared under this name in Cocktail Guide and Ladies' Companion *by Crosby Gaige, published in 1941.*

3 dashes of Angostura orange bitters
¼ ounce La Muse Verte absinthe
½ ounce Tempus Fugit crème de violette
¾ ounce La Quintinye Blanc vermouth
1¾ ounces Hayman's Royal Dock navy strength gin
Lemon twist, orange twist, for garnish

In a mixing glass, combine the bitters, absinthe, crème de violette, vermouth, and gin, and fill with ice. Stir the mixture and strain into a chilled Nick & Nora glass. Express the lemon and orange twists over the drink in that order, then discard.

PHILADELPHIA JACK

TOM COLLINS

*If we must call it what it is, this is an her-*baceous, white negroni decked out with all kinds of alpine herbal intensity from the Bësk, Suze, and Sapin (pine liqueur). However, it's unique (and delicious) in that it's a stirred drink finished with tonic water, which provides a welcome prickly texture and hint of quinine-inflected bitterness.

–½ ounce Letherbee Bësk
–½ ounce Suze gentian liqueur
¾ ounce Cocchi Americano vermouth
¾ ounce Sapin 40
¼ ounce tonic water
Lemon twist, for garnish

In a mixing glass, combine the Bësk, Suze, vermouth, and Sapin 40, and fill with ice. Stir the mixture and strain into a chilled Nick & Nora glass. Top with the tonic. Express the lemon twist over the drink, then discard.

We often recommend the Tom Collins—a quenching, hydrating, lifting cocktail— as an alternative to a G&T or a beer. But people forget the correlation between the Tom Collins and Old Tom gin, which was almost certainly what would have been used at the time of the drink's invention. We think this works beautifully with a barrel-aged Old Tom like Ransom's.

½ ounce lemon juice
1 ounce Lemon Cordial (page 177)
2 ounces Ransom's Barrel-Aged
   Old Tom gin
Soda water
Orange flag (a maraschino cherry
   skewered onto an orange wedge),
   for garnish

To a Boston tin or cobbler shaker, add the lemon juice, cordial, and gin. Fill the shaker with ice, cover, and shake vigorously. Fine strain the mixture into an ice-filled collins glass. Top with soda and garnish with an orange flag.

NEGRONI

We have thoughts. At the time we opened, the negroni, like the Last Word, was one of those classics so widely adopted by society at large as to become somewhat hackneyed and cliché. Despite its overexposure, the negroni's popularity has held up, a testament to the brilliance of the formula and proving it's no flash in the pan. However, the early years of the negroni were challenging, as the drink was often rendered heavy, sweet, and alcoholic—a bludgeon, not a wand. Bartenders often employed sweet and heavy Torino vermouths (like Carpano Antica formula) or people tried to substitute lesser aperitivi for Campari. At the end of the day, the negroni in its truest form can only be as written: equal parts, including Campari proper. However, the drink is infinitely improved when the vermouth is lighter, say with Cinzano or Dolin, and some bitters have been added. The gin should be a London Dry. The negroni is also often understirred—neither cold enough, nor diluted enough. Think elegance: It's a rocks drink you have to treat like an up drink.

> 3 dashes of Angostura orange bitters
> 1 ounce Cinzano Rossa vermouth
> 1 ounce Campari
> 1 ounce Beefeater gin
> Orange twist, for garnish

In a mixing glass, combine the bitters, vermouth, Campari, and gin, and fill with ice. Stir the mixture and strain into an ice-filled rocks glass. Garnish with an orange twist, inserted on the ice.

GIMLET

Our interest in the wonderfully simple, classic, and unfailingly delicious gimlet came via one of its few ingredients: lime cordial. A great gimlet is a strong exhortation to make your own cordials. Maison Premiere, like most bars, makes its own orgeat and grenadine. But, to our knowledge, few other bars make cordials. Bar director Will Elliott began experimenting with them and quickly became enamored. Made with both the juice and peel of a citrus fruit, the cordial becomes more than either alone—it's a concentrated, focused expression of the whole fruit that mere juice or a twist can't provide. (See our cordial recipe on page 177.) In many of his drinks, he started bolstering citrus juice with the cordial of the same fruit and found they became more intense, defined, and memorable cocktails.

A gimlet should just be cordial and gin. (Rose's Lime, the classic gimlet ingredient, is nothing but an overly saccharine cordial.) Our cordial is pure intensity. The drink comes to your choice: on the rocks or up.

> ½ ounce lime juice
> 1 ounce Lime Cordial (page 177)
> 2 ounces Hayman's navy strength gin

To a Boston tin or cobbler shaker, add the lime juice, cordial, and gin. Fill the shaker with ice, cover, and shake vigorously. Fine strain the mixture into an ice-filled rocks glass or chilled coupe.

HIGH CHICAGO

A study in the orange of beta-carotene, this original cocktail uses orange bitters, orange curaçao, mastiha (a Greek spirit that tastes like the core of a carrot), and apricot eau-de-vie. It's vegetal but also ethereal. A spray of carrot eau-de-vie finishes it appropriately.

4 dashes of Angostura orange bitters
¼ teaspoon kümmel
1 teaspoon Suze gentian liqueur
½ ounce Pierre Ferrand orange curaçao
½ ounce Pineau de Charentes
¾ ounce mastiha
1 ounce Blume Marillen apricot eau-de-vie
Orange twist and a spray of Reisetbauer carrot
   eau-de-vie, for garnish

In a mixing glass, combine the bitters, kümmel, Suze, curaçao, Pineau de Charentes, mastiha, and apricot eau-de-vie, and fill with ice. Stir the mixture and strain into a Nick & Nora glass containing one large ice cube. Express an orange twist over the drink, then discard. Finish with a spray of carrot eau-de-vie.

LAST WORD

Overly popular at the outset of the cocktail renaissance, this truly delicious and magisterial classic now finds itself slightly underrated and forgotten. We find it brazenly revitalized, however, by the additions of navy strength gin and these new, different maraschinos: Vergnano or Bordiga. This is an up drink, but we also love it served tall with a topping of soda as a highball.

¾ ounce lime juice
¾ ounce green Chartreuse
¾ ounce Vergnano or Bordiga maraschino liqueur
¾ ounce Hayman's navy strength gin
Lime twist and cherry on a skewer, for garnish

To a Boston tin or cobbler shaker, add the lime juice, Chartreuse, maraschino liqueur, and gin. Fill the shaker with ice, cover, and shake vigorously. Fine strain into a Nick & Nora glass. Express a lime twist over the drink, then discard. Garnish with a cherry on a skewer.

Tropicalia

෧෨

Given its Brooklyn digs and suit-wearing staff, Maison Premiere may not strike one as an enthusiastic purveyor of fruity, florid tropical drinks. And this is in one sense true. But on the other hand, we have reasons for our flirtation with the tropics, beginning with our primary geographical influence.

New Orleans is not a tropical city, but it faces the Caribbean, to which it has historically served as a maritime gateway. Its hot, steamy climate, featuring plentiful summertime rain, nurtures the same kind of flora one finds in latitudes to the south: exotic flowers, creeping vines, and fruiting shrubs.

And while Maison was originally built vaguely in the New York speakeasy vibe popular of its era, it has evolved. Construction of the garden in 2013—and its lush, backyard New Orleans feel—demanded a new kind of cocktail. So, we looked to the green, manicured, Anglophile drinks featured here under "Garden Cocktails" (page 117). But we also opened ourselves up to the tropics and their tiki derivations. Rum fits beautifully into our ethos, too—it is historical (far more prevalent in America's early days than whiskey), complex, and multifarious—all qualities we revere. Furthermore, tropical drinks respect the art of garnishing, so popular before Prohibition and which we have endeavored to restore.

Finally, while tropical drinks may run against the perceived Maison grain, let us also remember the most important thing—they're simply fun to drink. Sazeracs and Manhattans and martinis conjure a sort of weary urbanity that we appreciate (and experience). But Mais Tais and Piña Coladas and Jungle Birds are the kinds of drinks you have on vacation, and connote a joyous sense of adventure and seafaring worldliness.

DAIQUIRI

Starting somewhere in the early 2010s, the daiquiri quietly but suddenly came back into vogue among New York bartenders. Some of the resurgence may have been linked to the importing boom, which saw a raft of new, interesting rums flooding the market. A couple of influential bartenders became obsessed with perfecting the drink, which, despite its somewhat chintzy pop-culture reputation, is an extremely elegant and natively complex drink that rewards precision at every step. Our version stays true to the original formula but plays with the fine-tuning. The drink traditionally calls for a Cuban rum, which wasn't available at the time. While we were obsessed with rhum agricole and wanted to use it in the drink, we realized that a full two-ounce portion was too aggressively vegetal, so we balanced it with the easygoing Santa Teresa and never looked back. We also experimented with how to balance the sugar and acid. The original requirement of three-quarters of an ounce of lime juice didn't provide enough zing, so we bumped it up to a full ounce, while shrinking the sugar addition to just half an ounce but using a more concentrated two-to-one simple syrup. Finally, we got it right—a taut daiquiri with strong, clear flavors that is nevertheless perfectly balanced on the boundary between sharp and sweet.

> ½ ounce Rich Simple Syrup (page 175)
> 1 ounce lime juice
> 1 ounce Santa Teresa rum
> 1 ounce Neisson rhum agricole
> Thin, skewered lime wheel, Angostura bitters,
>   for garnish

To a Boston tin or cobbler shaker, add the simple syrup, lime juice, rum, and rhum agricole. Fill the shaker with ice, cover, and shake vigorously, a bit longer than you normally do. Strain into a chilled coupe. Garnish with a thin-sliced, skewered lime wheel dashed with a couple of drops of bitters.

MP JUNGLE BIRD

This is an adaption of an adaption. The original, one of the first tiki drinks to contain a bitter liqueur, hails from the 1970s and Kuala Lumpur's Aviary Bar. This cocktail received new life in 2010 when Giuseppe González, a bartender at New York's Painkiller (now closed), improved the jungle bird by making it with blackstrap rum, whose dense molasses character provided the depth the drink had been lacking. At Maison, we enrich it further with a funky pot stilled Jamaican rum for maximum flavor impact. The garnish, which features a wedge of Campari-soaked pineapple, has an origami-like precision. Soak the pineapple in Campari for twelve to twenty-four hours, then use the Campari in the drink.

–½ ounce Saline Solution (page 176)
½ ounce Demerara Simple Syrup (page 175)
–¾ ounce lime juice
+1 ounce pineapple juice
–¾ ounce Campari
¾ ounce Hamilton Pot Still Black rum
1 ounce Cruzan Black Strap rum
Campari-soaked pineapple wedge, fanned pineapple
    leaf skewered with cherry, for garnish

In a Boston tin shaker, combine the saline, simple syrup, lime juice, pineapple juice, Campari, and rums, and add about a cup of crushed ice. Shake until the ice has completely melted, then pour directly into an ice-filled rocks glass. Garnish with the pineapple wedge and leaf. (For the origami garnish, see photograph.)

MP MAI TAI

We love what we call "rum splits," meaning that instead of just using the one generic rum called for in the original recipe, we divide that portion among different styles of rums to achieve a more compelling, complex, and layered profile. Here, we use four different rums, which we mix ahead of time into a blend we call the Maison Premiere Mai Tai. The Hamilton Jamaican rum provides pot stilled funk; the Cruzan Black Strap lays a dark, molasses-driven base; the Santa Teresa layers on a buttery, rich softness; and a full ounce of La Favorite Coeur d'Ambre rhum agricole sharpens it all up with its herbaceous top notes. We don't make a lot of the modifiers we use in drinks, but we do love our homemade orgeat, which is produced with rose flower water, toasted almonds, and almond milk.

¾ ounce Maison Orgeat (page 176)
1 ounce lime juice
+¼ ounce Cruzan Black Strap rum
+¼ ounce Hamilton Pot Still Black rum
½ ounce Santa Teresa rum
1 ounce La Favorite Coeur d'Ambre rhum agricole
½ ounce Pierre Ferrand orange curaçao
Mint bouquet, Angostura bitters, edible pansy, orange
    flag (a maraschino cherry skewered onto an orange
    wedge), parasol, 1 short toddy straw, for garnish

In a Boston tin shaker, combine the orgeat, lime juice, rums, and curaçao with 1 cup of crushed ice. Give a short, vigorous shake, then dump the drink and ice into a poco grande glass. Garnish with a mint bouquet sprinkled with bitters, an edible pansy, an orange flag, a parasol, and the straw.

MAISON PIÑA COLADA

Sneer if you like, but this drink should be irresistible to all who lack a coconut allergy. When well made it's simply that delicious, no matter how your impression of it may have been colored by a family vacation to Club Med or reruns of *The Love Boat.* Our version, besides being served impressively in a hollowed-out coconut shell branded with our logo, is somewhat straightforward. But our two coconut syrups—one toasted, the other untoasted—give it a dimension you don't taste in other versions. Pimento dram is also known as allspice dram. We use a brand called St. Elizabeth.

1 teaspoon pimento dram
¾ ounce Maison Coconut Syrup (page 176)
¾ ounce Maison Toasted Coconut Syrup (page 176)
1 ounce lime juice
1 ounce pineapple juice
2 ounces Santa Teresa rum
Finely shredded toasted coconut, lime peel,
   2 cinnamon sticks, one grated on a Microplane,
   spray of Hamilton navy strength rum, mint bouquet,
   2 straws, for garnish

In a Boston tin shaker, combine the pimento dram, coconut syrups, lime juice, pineapple juice, and rum, and add 1 cup of crushed ice. Give a quick, vigorous shake and dump the drink and remaining ice into a hollowed-out coconut (see photograph). Garnish with the finely shredded toasted coconut, lime peel, and grated cinnamon stick. Spray the navy strength rum over the top. Insert a cinnamon stick, mint bouquet, and the straws.

USS BOMBER

Tall, glistening with crushed ice, and in brilliant shades of red, white, and blue, this unique cocktail is perfect for summer in the back garden. We promote it on American holidays of note—Derby Day(!), Memorial Day, Fourth of July, and Labor Day—when we festoon the bar with antique American flags and hire an old-timey brass band for live music. The whole place looks straight out of a 1940s film.

As for the drink, blue curaçao is of course not taken seriously by cocktail revivalists. But, Jesse, the bartender who created this drink, and Maxwell Britten weren't aiming for gravitas, instead desiring to maximize the patriotic visual effect, which they did. Along the way, they realized you could use any clear spirit in the drink you want, and it works. So, as with the toddy, customers call their spirit. We don't keep it on the menu for long, but it's always popular when we revive it.

1 ounce coconut milk
1 ounce lemon juice
¼ ounce Suze gentian liqueur
1 ounce clear spirit of choice, such as vodka, gin,
   or rum
¾ ounce blue curaçao
Peychaud's bitters
3 pineapple leaves, 1 red-and-white-striped straw,
   for garnish

Build all ingredients except for the blue curaçao and the bitters in a tall pilsner glass filled with crushed ice. Swizzle gently to combine. Carefully pour the curaçao so that it sits on top, and then, using a barspoon, gently nudge the ice to work the curaçao down until it forms a layer above the original drink. Now top with crushed ice and dash the Peychaud's bitters on top to form the red layer. Garnish with the pineapple leaves and the straw.

MISSIONARY'S DOWNFALL

"What one rum can't do, three rums can" is a quote allegedly issued by *Donn Beach, aka Don* the Beachcomber, aka the godfather of tiki. He also happens to be the inventor of this suggestively named cocktail. Ironically, in his original 1930s recipe for this drink, which calls for only one rum, he didn't follow his own dictum. We, however, did. Tripling a spirit in order to create complex layers of flavor is a technique we've used before in the sherry cobbler and mai tai. In true tiki fashion, this is a drink with a surfeit of ingredients, which we only exacerbate here. In the end, we hope you find it worthwhile. We surely do, as this is yet another tropical tiki drink whose complexity and sophistication belie its sunny brightness. You'll find that the mint and pineapple supply the high tones, the aged rums bring umami and depth, and the lemony acidity holds it all together. We serve this in what we call a bamboo collins glass—a tall glass with segmented bulges to mimic a bamboo trunk—but it works just as well in a regular collins glass.

¾ ounce lemon juice
1 ounce pineapple juice
¼ ounce Honey Syrup (page 177)
1 teaspoon crème de menthe
½ ounce Marie Brizard Apry apricot liqueur
¾ ounce El Dorado 3-year-old rum
½ ounce El Dorado 151 rum
¾ ounce Rhum J.M VSOP
2 small bunches of mint leaves
Mint bouquet, strips of lime peel, honeycomb,
    carnation flowers, and Osmanthus flowers,
    for garnish

To a Boston tin shaker, add the lemon juice, pineapple juice, honey syrup, crème de menthe, apricot liqueur, rums, and one bunch of mint, then set aside. Prepare a collins glass by gently muddling a handful of mint in the bottom of the glass. Then, on top of the mint, add crushed ice to three-quarters of the way to the top. Now, return to the shaker, fill it with ice cubes, and shake vigorously, then strain over the crushed ice. Insert a straw and garnish with a mint bouquet, strips of lime peel, honeycomb, carnation flowers, and Osmanthus flowers.

PISCO SOUR

DARK 'N' STORMY

Inseparably associated with its countries of origin, Chile and Peru, the pisco sour is seen as a niche drink to each country rather than the universal classic it could be. But because we get a lot of South American tourists, we are always ready to make one and do take the drink seriously. Indeed, it's interesting because the pisco sour is not niche at all—it's a classic sour. We add not only Angostura bitters but also Angostura orange bitters and orange flower water to amplify the floral high tones of pisco. Americans forget this drink, but they shouldn't—it's scrumptious.

> 3 dashes of Angostura bitters
> 3 dashes of Angostura orange bitters
> 3 drops of orange flower water
> ½ ounce cane syrup
> ¾ ounce lemon juice
> 1¾ ounces Capurro pisco
> Lemon twist, for garnish

To a Boston tin or cobbler shaker, add the two bitters, orange flower water, cane syrup, lemon juice, and pisco, cover, and dry shake. Now fill the shaker with ice, cover again, and shake vigorously. Strain the mixture into an ice-filled stemmed sour glass or wineglass. Express the lemon twist over the drink, then discard.

Legally, to call this drink a Dark 'n' Stormy, it must include Gosling's rum, which has trademarked the name. But nothing stipulates Gosling's must be the only rum in the drink, so we give it the "rum split" treatment, by supplementing Gosling's dark rum with a float of the even more potent and declarative Cruzan Black Strap rum. This is a phenomenal drink when made well, marrying depth, full-throated character, and a refreshing wispiness able to cut the oppressiveness of even the hottest summer day.

> ¾ ounce Ginger Syrup (page 175)
> 1 ounce lime juice
> 1¾ ounces Gosling's rum
> Ginger beer, such as Boylan's, or ale
> ¼ ounce Cruzan Black Strap rum
> Lime wheel, 1 tall straw, for garnish

To a Boston tin or cobbler shaker, add the ginger syrup, lime juice, and Gosling's rum. Fill the shaker with ice, cover, and shake vigorously. Fine strain the mixture into an ice-filled collins glass. Top with ginger beer or ale to just below the rim. Now float the Cruzan Black Strap rum on top. Garnish with a lime wheel and the straw.

Syrups and Cordials

Here are the recipes for add-ins that take ordinary cocktails to the next level. To ensure stability and preservation, we add an ounce of vodka to our syrups per quart.

GINGER SYRUP (1:1)

> 1 part ginger juice (see Note)
> 1 part superfine sugar
> 2 cinnamon sticks

In a pot set over medium heat, combine equal parts ginger juice and superfine sugar. Bring the mixture to a low simmer and stir until the sugar has dissolved. Remove the pot from the heat. Add the cinnamon sticks and let sit for 20 minutes. The syrup can be stored in the refrigerator for two weeks.

NOTE • To make ginger juice, take whole, unpeeled ginger and run it through a juice extractor. Skim off any scum. Run once through a fine-mesh strainer to remove any particulate matter.

SIMPLE SYRUP (1:1)

> 1 part sugar
> 1 part water

In a pot, combine the sugar and water in equal parts and stir until the sugar has dissolved, but do not heat the pot. Warm to hot water may be used to help the sugar dissolve. The syrup can be stored in the refrigerator for two weeks.

RICH SIMPLE SYRUP (2:1)

> 2 parts sugar
> 1 part water

In a pot, combine the sugar and water and stir until the sugar has dissolved, but do not heat the pot. Warm to hot water may be used to help the sugar dissolve. The syrup can be stored in the refrigerator for two weeks.

RASPBERRY SYRUP

> 6 ounces raspberries
> 1 cup Rich Simple Syrup (above)
> 6 drops of rose flower water

Add the raspberries to the simple syrup. Add the rose flower water and blend until smooth. Strain the mixture through a fine-mesh strainer. The syrup can be stored in the refrigerator for two weeks.

DEMERARA SIMPLE SYRUP (2:1)

> 2 parts Demerara sugar
> 1 part water

In a pot set over medium heat, combine equal parts Demerara sugar and water. Bring the mixture to a low simmer and stir until the sugar has dissolved. Remove the pot from the heat and allow to cool. The syrup can be stored in the refrigerator for two weeks.

GENTIAN SYRUP

1 cup sugar
1 cup water
1 grapefruit peel
¼ ounce gentian root

In a small pot set over medium heat, combine the sugar, water, and grapefruit peel, and stir until the sugar is dissolved.

Remove the pot from the heat and add the gentian root. Steep the gentian for ten minutes and then strain the mixture through a fine-mesh strainer. The syrup can be stored in the refrigerator for two weeks.

SALINE SOLUTION

2 parts water
1 part salt

In a pot or bowl, combine the water and salt. Mix until the salt is dissolved. The solution can be stored in the refrigerator for two weeks.

MAISON ORGEAT

8 ounces slivered almonds
1 quart unsweetened almond milk
1 quart sugar
1 teaspoon kosher salt

Place the nuts on a sheet tray and bake at 350°F, stirring every couple of minutes until the almonds reach a deep golden brown, approximately 8 minutes. In a large pot set over medium heat, add the almond milk and sugar and heat through. Add the toasted almonds and salt, then simmer the mixture for 45 minutes, stirring occasionally. Strain through a fine-mesh strainer and then cool the liquid rapidly in an ice bath. The orgeat can be stored in the refrigerator for several weeks.

YIELDS ABOUT 1½ QUARTS

MAISON COCONUT SYRUP

3 parts coconut syrup (such as Giffard)
1 part coconut milk

In a pot set over low heat, combine the coconut syrup and coconut milk and stir until well mixed. Allow to cool. The syrup can be stored in the refrigerator for several weeks.

MAISON TOASTED COCONUT SYRUP

1 quart coconut milk
2 cups toasted coconut flakes
2 cups sugar
1 tablespoon salt
Peels of 3 limes
1 ounce Kalani coconut rum liqueur

In a large pot over medium heat, combine the coconut milk and flakes, sugar, salt, and lime peels. Simmer for 45 minutes. Strain through a fine-mesh strainer and add the rum liqueur. The syrup can be stored in the refrigerator for three weeks.

YIELDS JUST OVER 1 QUART

MAISON 7-SPICE CHAI SYRUP

2 cups water
2 cups sugar
1½ tablespoons whole cloves
1 star anise
1½ teaspoons ground allspice
1 cinnamon stick
1 tablespoon black pepper
½ cup roughly chopped ginger
1½ teaspoons ground cardamom
1½ teaspoons kosher salt
Peel of 2 oranges

In a medium pot set over medium heat, combine the water, sugar, cloves, star anise, allspice, cinnamon stick, black pepper, ginger, cardamom, salt, and orange peels. Bring to a simmer and cook for 30 minutes. Strain the mixture through a fine-mesh strainer. Express and discard the orange peel while the mixture cools. The syrup can be stored in the refrigerator for two weeks.

YIELDS ABOUT 1½ QUARTS

LIME CORDIAL

Zest of 3 limes
1 cup sugar
1 cup lime juice
½ ounce vodka

In a container with a lid, combine the lime zest and sugar and leave covered at room temperature for 24 hours, or overnight, agitating intermittently. After the marination period, add the lime juice and vodka, and stir until thoroughly mixed and the sugar is dissolved. Strain the liquid through a fine-mesh strainer and chill. The cordial can be stored in the refrigerator for a month.

LEMON CORDIAL

Zest of 3 lemons
1 cup sugar
1 cup lemon juice
½ ounce vodka

In a container with a lid, combine the lemon zest and sugar and leave covered at room temperature for 24 hours, or overnight, agitating intermittently. After the marination period, add the lemon juice and vodka to the mixture and stir until thoroughly combined and the sugar is dissolved. Strain the liquid through a fine-mesh strainer and chill. The cordial can be stored in the refrigerator for a month.

MAISON GRENADINE

8 ounces pomegranate juice, such as POM Wonderful
½ cup Sugar In The Raw or Demerara sugar
1 ounce pomegranate molasses, such as Al Wadi
Peel of 1 orange

In a small pot set over low heat, combine the pomegranate juice and sugar, and stir until the sugar dissolves. Do not allow the mixture to boil.

Remove the pot from the heat and add the pomegranate molasses. Express and then discard the orange peel. Chill and store. The grenadine can be stored in the refrigerator for two weeks.

PASSION FRUIT SYRUP

1 part passion fruit puree
½ part grenadine
½ part Demerara sugar
2 parts coconut syrup (such as Giffard)

In a pot set over low heat, combine the passion fruit puree, grenadine, sugar, and coconut syrup, and stir until the sugar is dissolved. Cool and store the mixture. The syrup can be stored in the refrigerator for two weeks.

HONEY SYRUP (1:1)

1 part hot water
1 part honey

In a pot set over low heat, combine equal amounts of hot water and honey. Stir until the honey is dissolved. The syrup can be stored in the refrigerator for a month.

3.

ABSINTHE:
THE SONG OF
THE GREEN
FAIRIE

TO INCLUDE:

the tumultuous, sometimes tawdry history

of an ethereal spirit; how to drink it; proper

absinthe service and cocktails

Thus we have one important point settled, namely, the Frenchman does not go to a café for the sake of drinking, nor does he drink at the café for the sake of drinking much less because he is thirsty: he drinks simply because he wants to go to the café.

—Theodore Child, "Characteristic Parisian Cafés,"
Harper's Magazine, April 1889

MAGINE STROLLING THE BOULEVARDS OF PARIS IN THE 1880s. It's early summer, just after five in the evening—*l'heure verte,* the green hour, so called for the prolific amount of absinthe gracing every table—and the indoor cafés are filling up because already the sidewalk tables are crowded and noisy.

You are a boulevardier, one who strolls the streets to see and be seen, to survey Paris through its suddenly flourishing café society. Each café is different, with its own clientele and culture. One spot is populated with stockbrokers and financiers in topcoats and top hats. The neighboring café features military and naval officers, all drinking the green spirit, which they developed a habit of while serving in the colonies, where it was issued as a mild antibacterial. The next café has journalists and businessmen; the next is an international hub for all manner of foreign visitors and expats. Finally, up on the great hill of Montmartre, you get to the true bohemian places, where the poets, painters, musicians, sculptors, actors, and actresses congregate at all hours to drink and argue about art and philosophy.

All of this is of course fueled by alcohol, much of it green. *L'heure verte* lasts from five until seven, at which time Parisians disappear somewhere for dinner before descending back onto the boulevards from nine until the night and *la fée verte* (the green fairie) take them away again.

Wormwood

Anise

Fennel

What Is Absinthe?

AND AN EXCEEDINGLY BRIEF HISTORY OF THE SPIRIT UP UNTIL THE PRESENT MOMENT, PLUS A FEW LESSONS TO BE LEARNED FROM ITS RISE AND FALL AND RISE AGAIN.

ORIGINS • The name absinthe derives from the Latin *absinthium*, as in the plant *Artemisia absinthium*, otherwise known as wormwood. Carl Linnaeus named the plant in his 1753 taxonomy *Species Plantarum*, but the use of wormwood in spirits goes back millennia, to at least the Egyptians. With a sort of minty, menthol taste, wormwood is exceedingly bitter and has been used medicinally and as a flavoring agent. The aromatized wine vermouth gets its name and bitterness from the addition of wormwood.

The modern spirit absinthe has been popularly attributed to Pierre Ordinaire, a French doctor living just over the border in far west Switzerland, who in the 1790s practiced distilling various tonics and elixirs. He paired wormwood with, among other botanicals, anise and fennel to create absinthe's distinctive licorice flavor. Distillation of wormwood, as opposed to steeping, allowed the preservation of its flavor without introducing its bitterness. He also infused the spirit after distillation with other botanicals that provided its signature green color. Ordinaire's recipe changed hands after his death, ending up on the French side of the border in the town of Pontarlier, where it was distilled commercially by a man named Pernod in 1805. Pernod would go on to become the largest absinthe company in the world, and its absinthe is still available today.

TAKEAWAY • Wild herbs, flowers, and vegetables are good for us.

THE RISE • In the nineteenth century absinthe's popularity grew steadily. By the 1840s, the French Foreign Legion stationed in Algeria was given rations of absinthe for its antiseptic qualities. The enthusiasm the troops developed for it returned with them to civilian life, spreading a taste for absinthe throughout the country.

As the Industrial Revolution fueled the growth of cities, absinthe became the drink of choice for the large set of younger people who moved to them. Underemployed, anti-bourgeoisie, and somewhat set adrift, this group assumed a countercultural pose and indulged their predilections for drinking, hanging out in cafés, making art, writing, talking, etc. They became known as the bohemians (after nomadic itinerants from the Bohemia region of Central Europe) and fueled the rise of café society and modern art in places like Paris and Lyon. Absinthe was said to proffer a sort of lucid high. As all alcoholic beverages do, it lowers inhibitions, yet it uniquely offers a certain simultaneous clarity of mind, which is why it appealed so powerfully to artists and writers. In this context, absinthe became a multifaceted symbol—of societal decay, of counterculture, and of creativity and art. In 1805, at the beginning of the century, Pernod's first distillery reportedly could produce about sixteen liters of spirit a day. A century later France was drinking thirty-six million liters a year.

Absinthe made its way to the United States most prominently through the French-founded port city of New Orleans. The city's Francophilia is well known, but it also managed to adopt the bohemian ribaldry of Paris. Absinthe was warmly welcomed there. In 1874 a Catalan bartender opened his own bar, called the Absinthe Room because demand was high for the spirit, which he served in the Parisian way, diluted by drip and in his famous frappé. By 1890, the bar was called the Old Absinthe House.

TAKEAWAY • *Laissez les bons temps roulez!*

THE DOWNFALL • Despite being a hugely popular spirit enjoyed in multiple countries, absinthe had a swift and shocking downfall that led to its ban. In many ways it was a victim of its own success.

In France, the boom in café culture and drinking created an epidemic of alcoholism. Wine and other spirits were age-old and sacred, so absinthe became the scapegoat. One very influential doctor even diagnosed an illness of absinthe overconsumption, calling it *absinthism* and claiming it resulted in insanity, epilepsy, and birth defects.

Concurrently, profiteers began producing cheap knockoffs. Often these fake absinthes contained heavy metals and poisonous chemicals, yet they still found their way legally into the market because absinthe was unregulated (unlike, say, Cognac or Burgundy). The victims were the poorest and most desperate of alcoholics.

The medical diagnosis of absinthe drinkers and the ravages on society wrought by drinking played right into the hands of the growing temperance movement, which would become a powerful force in the early twentieth century in many countries.

Finally, absinthe had made a powerful enemy of the wine world, which was trying to come back from phylloxera, the root louse that devastated French vineyards in the late nineteenth century. Large winemakers wanted their market dominance back and tacitly joined forces with the temperance movement and the medical establishment to demonize absinthe in print and politically.

TAKEAWAY • Don't shop in dark alleys.

THE MURDER • All that was needed to drop the guillotine on absinthe was a salacious crime, and 1905 provided it. In Switzerland, farmer Jean Lanfray got into an argument with his pregnant wife and ended up shooting her and their two daughters before shooting himself. Earlier in the day he had consumed two glasses of absinthe. But he had also drunk at least six glasses of wine, several brandies, a couple of crèmes de menthe, and was generally known to be a raging alcoholic. Nonetheless, news of the crime spread, with the press dubbing it "the absinthe murder." (He failed in killing himself; the next day he remembered none of it.) At his trial, Lanfray tried to blame absinthism and brought in a doctor to testify on that line. He lost the case and hanged himself in prison three days later.

TAKEAWAY • Drink only in moderation.

THE BANS • The Lanfray murders gave absinthe detractors the sensationalized fulcrum they needed to ban absinthe. After all, who was there to defend it but a bunch of underemployed bohemians? Switzerland banned the spirit in 1910. The United States outlawed it under an amendment to the Pure Food and Drugs Act in 1912, noting its deleterious properties. Following suit, France banned it in 1914, though it hardly seemed as important as it might have, given that World War I broke out that summer, slamming the door shut not just on the absinthe era but on the Belle Epoque.

TAKEAWAY • Crisis-management fail!

THE INTERIM • Not all countries banned absinthe; for instance, it remained legal in the UK and Spain. But France and Switzerland produced almost all of the world's absinthe, so there was really no product to satisfy what small demand existed. In France, wormwood-less anise-flavored spirits called pastis arrived to fill the void, but, compared to artisanal absinthe, they were overly sweet and simplistic.

In the latter decades of the twentieth century, absinthe lived on mostly as a thing of legend. During the counterculture moment of the '60s and '70s, a mystique developed around absinthe's so-called ability to induce hallucinations and creativity and euphoria, but there was no absinthe around to sample, so it existed notoriously in the collective imagination as a risqué substance.

TAKEAWAY • Nothing like the real thing.

THE RETURN • Existing in modern popular culture only as a forbidden drug, absinthe had a mystique that began attracting more serious inquiry. Starting in the late '90s, various scientific investigations into absinthe and its supposed psychoactive properties debunked the old myths.

In the ensuing few years, people in different countries conducted separate and independent chemical analyses of surviving bottles of pre-ban absinthe. In the United States that person was Ted Breaux, a laboratory chemist from New Orleans. Using a mass spectrometer—a tool that can analyze and identify component parts within various substances to microscopic precision (parts per million)—he looked into samples of pre-ban absinthe and found thujone (the dangerous compound in question) in amounts so tiny that it could pose no danger. In some absinthes he found no thujone at all. The upshot was that high-quality, well-made absinthe contains nothing harmful or even psychoactive.

While bans were being lifted in Europe, the United States held firm until 2007, when Breaux and his group successfully lobbied the government to allow the import, distribution, and sale of absinthe for the first time since 1912. That opened the floodgates to not only further imports but also absinthe distillation in the US, which has produced some marvelous examples. Any bartender at Maison Premiere will be happy to introduce you to our list.

TAKEAWAY • Science!

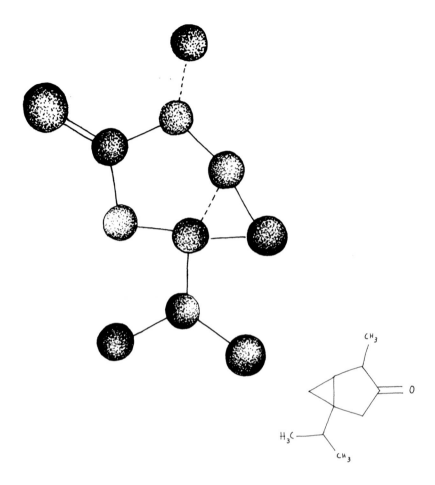

You're Not Hallucinating

BUT YOU MAY BE FEELING THE INEXPLICABLE EUPHORIA OF THE ABSINTHE "HIGH"

The chemical scapegoated for causing absinthe to be toxic and hallucinatory is called thujone. It's found in wormwood and many other plants, including tarragon and sage, and tastes of menthol. While thujone has not been shown to be psychoactive in any way or in any concentration, it's true that at extremely high doses, it can be a toxic convulsant. However, even remotely high enough concentrations of thujone are never found in absinthe. Europe allows up to 35 milligrams per liter of thujone in absinthe, while the United States allows only 10 milligrams. These limits have not posed a problem to any absinthe's legal standing, as very few absinthes ever even approach the US limit.

While you won't be hallucinating, alongside any buzz you feel from alcohol, you may feel a potent sense of clarity. Some call it lucidity; others call it euphoria. Either way, whatever this feeling is, it has never been scientifically documented or proven, yet it appears so often in anecdotal accounts of absinthe inebriation that it must be taken seriously. It is after all why absinthe was called the Muse and the Green Faerie— somehow it stimulates thinking and creativity, opening pathways that seemed to be shut during sobriety and confused during normal drunkenness. Perhaps it's caused by the combination of absinthe's heady botanicals with high-proof spirit.

This lovely feeling persists for a while during absinthe drinking but will eventually give way to just plain old inebriation, or worse. As Oscar Wilde famously wrote, "After the first glass of absinthe you see things as you wish they were. After the second you see them as they are not. Finally, you see things as they really are, and that is the most horrible thing in the world."

THE QUALITIES OF ABSINTHE WE SEEK, AND THE IMPORTANCE OF THE LOUCHE

DISTILLATION • Good absinthe is made through distillation and not maceration— a shortcut not as deadly as those taken in the nineteenth century but nevertheless a shortcut. In distillation, the botanicals are infused into neutral spirit and then redistilled one or two times, serving to extract the flavors and aromas without carrying forward the bitterness. Afterward, if the spirit is to be a green absinthe, a very short and light maceration of herbs (often including hyssop) are steeped like a teabag to add chlorophyll for the green hue.

By contrast, in macerated absinthes, botanicals would be steeped in high-proof spirit, which adds flavor and color but also bitterness. However, in reality, quantities of neutral spirit are often mixed with essential oils and finished with food coloring. These are fraught absinthes as are any derived from a kit you may order online that gives you the ingredients to mix at home. Avoid these.

HIGHER POWERS • Absinthe is traditionally a very strong, overproof spirit. This is why on our absinthe menu, we list the alcohol by volume percentage for each bottle; they run typically from 45 proof to around 68 proof. There's a reason for this unrestrained power. Absinthe is a tremendously aromatic and flavorful botanical spirit. The biggest contributors to an absinthe's flavor are oils, and these oils are soluble in ethanol, not water. So in order to carry a certain level of flavor, the ethanol concentration needs to be high enough.

THE LOUCHE • Good, high-proof absinthes are too strong to drink straight, really. Some people may do it and spout nonsense about masculinity and chest hair. But, honestly, drinking absinthe that strong doesn't do the spirit any favors and burns the tongue. These were made to be diluted.

As suggested earlier, to remain clear in the bottle absinthes have to be of a certain strength. As water is added, however, they gradually become cloudy, which is called louching. Clear absinthes turn a milky white, while green absinthes and pastis turn a cloudy green.

Louching in this way is a feature specifically of spirits containing anise oils. Below 50 proof, the clarity of an absinthe is jeopardized. Higher alcohol percentages provide insurance against these oil molecules falling out of suspension and turning the spirit cloudy. At lower alcohol percentages this can even happen if storage temperatures become too cold.

With regard to absinthe, the fascinating aspect of this phenomenon is that the liquid remains cloudy and will do so for months. Typically, when something precipitates out of a clear solution, the heavier liquid settles on the bottom, the way oil and vinegar will separate in a vinaigrette. To make oil and vinegar temporarily remain in solution, you must add energy via a furious whisking or a blender, or you can add an emulsifying agent like mustard or mayonnaise. But absinthe's louche requires no added energy or emulsifier. This mysterious effect has puzzled scientists, who unwisely called it the "ouzo effect" after the Greek anise-flavored spirit (it should have been called the "absinthe effect").

The importance of louching goes beyond diluting the alcoholic punch. Pulling those essential oil compounds out of suspension actually makes them more available to our noses and tongues, allowing us to enjoy all the complexities of good absinthe. The added water also helps to spread the absinthe thoroughly across the mouth and tongue, allowing it to connect with more of our taste receptors and enhancing the experience.

WHAT TO LOOK FOR AND OUR FAVORITE ABSINTHES

As with wine, complexity and balance are things we look for in a good absinthe. A well-made spirit will have harmonious and interesting flavors. It should have a broad, silky mouthfeel. And the flavors of anise and fennel and other botanicals should be clear and precise, suggesting sweetness, not bitterness. The spirit should be dry and bracing in its herbal freshness, like a mountain meadow in full bloom. A fine absinthe is the mark of a skilled and talented distiller, as it leaves nowhere—not under a fog of sugar nor in a cloud of synthetic flavors—to hide one's mistakes.

The best way to choose an absinthe, of course, is to taste it for yourself. In the absence of that opportunity, however, other resources exist, the best being the Wormwood Society, a nonprofit dedicated to educating and informing about absinthe. Founded in 2004 from a private tasting and discussion group of absinthe enthusiasts, the association has become global and maintains a highly informative and trustworthy website with a great deal of information, including reviews.

On that note, we at Maison Premiere know a thing or two about absinthe as well. Here are a few of our favorite American versions.

DELAWARE PHOENIX • This absinthe was made in a small town in the Catskills by the late Cheryl Lins, who discovered the spirit after reading a 2006 *New Yorker* article and ordered a couple of bottles from Europe (this was before the lifting of the ban). She absolutely loved it, but continuing to order from Europe was prohibitively expensive, so instead she bought a little copper pot still and taught herself how to make absinthe. Today her spirits—which can still be found in the market (at least for a while) and should be sought out—are powerful and soulful and delicious. Two versions exist. Meadow of Love was her "feminine" absinthe for its violet-derived florality, while Walton Waters is a more traditional formula that she described as "masculine."

ST. GEORGE ABSINTHE VERTE • After the ban was lifted in 2007, St. George Spirits of Alameda, California, was the first to market with its daring, no-holds-barred 60 percent ABV formula. This is not surprising if you know St. George's other spirits or its master distiller, Lance Winters, neither of which lack a point of view or the will to support it. Dry, powerful, and bracing, this absinthe is still an industry standard.

GERMAIN-ROBIN ABSINTHE SUPÉRIEURE • Made by hand in very small batches in Mendocino, California, this absinthe is a unique version of the form: absinthe blanche. Since it wasn't macerated with green botanicals, it's not green in color but rather a delicate off-white. Inherent sweetness comes from the apple-honey base distillate, and exotics like rose geranium and lemon balm assist the traditional wormwood and fennel. It's not easy being not-green!

Rituals and Protocols, How to Drink It

———

MAISON PREMIERE ABSINTHE SERVICE

One of the things we loved about absinthe from the beginning is that it was more than just another liquor. Not only did it come with a powerful legacy, it came with ritual. It came with ceremony, and in that it is unique among mainstream spirits. A ritual draws attention to the act of drinking, makes it significant and profound. Everything about Maison Premiere is about slowing down, escaping our mindless modern ricochet. Absinthe happened to be, in spirit form, the perfect embodiment of this idea.

As we knew from one of our inspirational guides, David Nathan-Maister's incredible *The Absinthe Encyclopedia*, "The 'ritual' is important—it is key to the fascination of absinthe. No other drink is traditionally consumed with such a carefully calibrated ceremony." He says that absinthe was never drunk rudely: "Even the poorest working man, in the roughest bar or café, would prepare his absinthe slowly and carefully."

Here are the elements you need to drink absinthe slowly and carefully:

ABSINTHE SPOON • The famous, usually decorative, slotted spoon that has been a signature absinthe accoutrement for centuries. It can stir a drink, but its main role is to sit across the mouth of the glass to support a sugar cube while allowing water to drip through it. You don't need an ornate museum piece to accomplish this at home; a simple fork will do. But if you are a regular absinthe drinker, a lovely spoon only adds to the refinement of the ritual.

PONTARLIER GLASS • This thick-stemmed, faceted glass dates back to the nineteenth century, and became synonymous with absinthe thanks to its appearance in a widely distributed advertisement for Pernod Absinthe, whose distillery was located in Pontarlier. Some Pontarlier glasses have an etched line to designate the proper pour. A regular absinthe drinker should own a set of these for ritual and the sake of tradition. For the occasional absinthe drinker at home, a wineglass serves just as well.

SUGAR CUBE (OPTIONAL) • First produced in the nineteenth century, sugar cubes are not as common today as they used to be but are still available. A standard C&H white sugar cube measures ⅝ inch per edge and contains fifteen calories. Sugar is indeed optional, though its addition has always been part of the ritual. Good absinthe, most people will agree, is not bitter. "A spoonful of sugar helps the medicine go down" does not apply. The tradition goes back to nineteenth-century France, when the liquor people consumed was often sweet. People then sometimes added two or three cubes to an absinthe. Rather—and we encourage you to try it—a dissolved sugar cube in a dose of absinthe doesn't add much sweetness. But it does alter the body and texture of the drink, often for the better, though how that is accomplished is difficult to articulate. As Nathan-Maister writes, "Generally sugar binds together otherwise disparate flavour elements and smooths out the drink, and it's primarily for this reason that absinthe was historically usually drunk with sugar . . . Absinthe with sugar added tastes rounder, and more unified." In our experience, this is accurate.

WATER • Water is crucial and should be as cold and as pure as possible. Every recommendation is for three to five parts water per one part absinthe. And that's a big range. The important part is that absinthe is diluted, and the addition is a huge part of the ritual. According to *The Absinthe Encyclopedia*, "true absintheurs used to take great care in adding the water, letting it fall drop by single drop onto the sugar cube, and then watching each individual drip cut a milky swathe through the peridot-green absinthe below. Seeing the drink gradually change colour was an important part of its attraction." We subscribe to this. Slow down, take your time. The gradual saturation with water accomplishes two things. The visual amalgamation of water and spirit creates a beautiful spectacle, as one watches opacity gradually take over the glass. And it also loses the aromatics slowly, allowing individual aromatic compounds to be released in a pleasurable sequence. Fountains accomplish dilution best, but you can pour by hand if you do it slowly, as Nathan-Maister explains: "Holding the carafe in a relaxed and stylish way high above the glass, and letting the water slowly drip out drop for drop is harder than you'd think, and was a much admired skill."

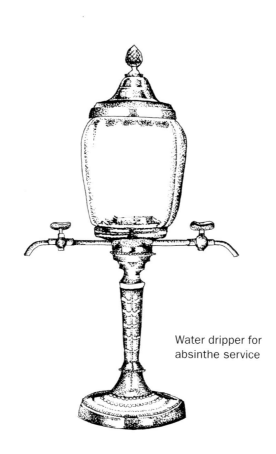

Water dripper for absinthe service

How We Serve Absinthe

Maison Premiere serves absinthe in three ways: diluted with water from the absinthe drip, in a frappé, and in cocktails.

MAISON PREMIERE DRIP SERVICE

An absinthe of the customer's choice, diluted with a steady drip of cold water from the absinthe fountain through a sugar cube. It takes a couple of minutes to prepare, but that's the point—to slow down and enjoy the beauty of the ritual. You can watch as the spirit at first takes the water, then begins to undulate, and finally begins to cloud. Absinthe is the core of our spirits program, so we have very precise service protocols. The commonly suggested dilution for most strong absinthes is three to five parts water to one part spirit. This service dilutes to about three-and-a-half or four to one. If and when the customer orders another absinthe, only the glass is removed. The saucer underneath it remains in place and a second saucer is placed atop it. This was the old French method of keeping track of a customer's absinthe tab.

ABSINTHE FRAPPÉ

This method of serving chilled absinthe was invented at the Old Absinthe House of New Orleans by its owner and barman Cayetano Ferrer in 1874 and became a staple of that bar and the city. The ingredients are hardly different from serving a drip, but the addition of crushed ice instead of water makes it perfectly refreshing on a hot, humid day.

FRAPPÉ SERVICE • Place a saucer before the customer. Add a short quarter ounce of Rich Simple Syrup (page 175) to a chilled Pontarlier glass. On top of that pour 1¼ ounces of absinthe. Fill the glass with crushed ice. Place one half of a tin shaker over the glass and gently shake until the tin begins to frost over, 15 to 20 seconds. Release the seal of the glass, and place the glass on the saucer. Pour the absinthe and ice back into the glass and top with a gentle mound of crushed ice. Garnish with a straw.

ABSINTHE COCKTAILS

Absinthe was a cornerstone of the original cocktail movement and remains so today in the classic cocktail movement. We offer some classic and original absinthe cocktails on the following pages. Given that we have mixed with it so much, we've included a number of principles and ideas about its uses here.

1. **A little goes a long way.** Be careful when mixing absinthe with other spirits. It's so powerfully flavored and at such a high degree of alcohol, it can easily overwhelm other elements in a concoction.

2. While a little does go a long way, **don't be afraid of a drop of absinthe.** Absinthe is indeed a dominant spirit, but a subtle, almost invisible addition can work wonders for a drink. It adds an element that you don't actually taste, but the drink would be less without. Our cocktail Future Days (page 142) and our Maison Stinger call for microadditions of absinthe.

3. **Tighten your screws.** Absinthe is briskly clean and dry, and it can bring those qualities to a drink that needs discipline. If you have a drink that's sort of loose or squirrelly, that seems to lack spine, try a dash of absinthe. It has the effect of a good wrench—it can tighten the joints, bolt things together.

4. **Be wary of brown spirits.** Of course, we all bow down before the almighty Sazerac, but in general and to our palate, absinthe doesn't often play well with brown spirits like whiskey and rum. Use accordingly.

5. **Gin is in.** Obviously, absinthe has a deep affinity for gin. While juniper and anise are separate flavors, they work well together, like caraway seeds in rye bread. Absinthe also works well with other herbal and floral spirits (e.g., some amari and piscos).

6. **Rinse and repeat.** As in the aforementioned Sazerac, an absinthe rinse inside a glass before adding the (usually) nonabsinthe-containing cocktail can create beguiling tension and contrast within a drink. We've seen a simple absinthe rinse lift an otherwise banal cocktail up to the sublime.

7. **Mind the louche.** Don't forget that if added to a drink that you will dilute (and this is most drinks), absinthe will still louche. This is a problem if you desire a clear drink. But it can also be spectacular, as in all manner of martini variations.

8. **Body building.** Especially in stirred absinthe drinks, where it can be a challenge to create body, use a wine-based ingredient to help flush it out. Vermouth, sherry, and even wine itself can work great alongside absinthe and introduce both body and finish to a drink that needs bolstering.

HOW WE DON'T SERVE ABSINTHE

AFLAME • Fire and alcohol just don't mix. This service of absinthe, also called the Bohemian method, is not practiced at Maison Premiere. We will not even prepare it upon request. Nevertheless, we'll describe it here, so you know what it is.

The Bohemian method involves the reckless act of lighting an absinthe-soaked sugar cube on fire and allowing it to melt into the glass below. Not only is it dangerous to introduce fire in the vicinity of a very high-proof spirit, but the practice is disingenuous. This method supposedly debuted in the Czech Republic in the 1980s and 1990s. Macerated absinthes of poor quality were available there at the time, an exotic experience for westerners visiting Prague in the early years after it emerged from communist control. Because they were macerated, these absinthes didn't louche, making pointless the French ritual of dripping water. So as an alternative, bartenders developed this parlor trick, which served to both entertain with a frisson of danger and also distract consumers from the fact that their off-putting absinthe didn't louche.

Drinking Absinthe at Home

If you have an absinthe fountain already, you don't need to read this. But if you don't, it's perfectly easy to make this at home with a pitcher or bottle of cold water. If you don't have a Pontarlier glass, a wineglass works very well, too. Just be sure not to add the water too quickly, so you can enjoy the louche.

HOW MUCH WATER TO ADD • This is purely a matter of taste and depends on the alcoholic strength of the absinthe you're drinking. Some like it stronger, some weaker. A common method is to add just enough water to louche the entire glass of absinthe, so that no layer of clear spirit remains. That would be enough water to take it down to just under 30 proof alcohol, meaning a drink that's a bit weaker than a standard 40 proof whiskey. But it's also perfectly fine to dilute the absinthe further, bringing it down to about 13 or 14 percent, about the strength of a glass of wine.

HOW TO ADD WATER GRACEFULLY • This is the trick few have figured out. The casual method would be to just shrug your shoulders and dump cold water from a carafe into the waiting glass of absinthe. The measured way would be to drop it via an eyedropper or, more crudely, a turkey baster. The classy way that honors the elegance of the absinthe ritual is to use an ornamental decanter with a precision pour spout. However, before you buy, consider the size and weight of this decanter. A larger, heavier pitcher will be much more difficult to control, and your wrist will fatigue. We therefore recommend a crystal wine decanter with a pewter or silver-plate top and pour spout. These antiques are neither uncommon nor expensive and make for beautiful additions to the absinthe ritual.

SUGAR OR NOT • Again, this is a matter of taste. Purists drinking high-quality absinthe will not usually add sugar, as a good spirit is not bitter and needs no help. But some people like a little sweetness. Certainly, in the nineteenth century, when the practice began, people were accustomed to drinking sweet liqueurs and sweetened their absinthe out of habit. But today, no one should be embarrassed. A cube of sugar in a dose of absinthe mildly rounds out the mouthfeel, helps its flavors to coalesce, and doesn't significantly or negatively alter the taste.

Maison Original and Classic Absinthe Cocktails

The pages that follow feature Maison Premiere's favorite absinthe cocktail recipes—new takes on century-old classics and original concoctions that feature the spirit—all written to be prepared in a home bar, no matter what kind of equipment you have on hand. Before making any cocktail, be sure to review the list of principles on page 194, and note the following explanations to the recipes.

COCKTAIL NOTES

1. A minus (–) or plus (+) sign before a measurement (such as –½ ounce) indicates a short or long version of the ingredient. It should be just a tad less or more than the precise amount.

2. The kind of ice is indicated, unless it is served up (without ice), which is also indicated.

3. When a recipe instructs you to garnish with a discarded lemon twist, it means you should express a twist over the cocktail and then discard it.

CHRYSANTHEMUM

Making its first appearance in Hugo Ensslin's 1916 Recipes for Mixed Drinks, *the* Chrysanthemum was ripe for reimagining in 2010s Brooklyn. It's a lovely and early example of low-ABV drinking, a style growing in popularity in recent years. Since Maison Premiere is at its core an absinthe bar, we decided the selection of absinthe in our rendition must be thoughtfully chosen. Germain-Robin is what we call an "outlier" absinthe: though it follows all the rules of proper absinthe production, the end result yields a very unique profile, with heavy aromatics of mint, fresh fennel, and even rose. This adds finessed aromatics and finish to a powerfully herbal "up" drink that can often tend toward the two-dimensional. This recipe is adapted from *The Savoy Cocktail Book* by Harry Craddock, originally published in 1930.

6 drops of aromatic bitters
–½ ounce Germain-Robin absinthe
¾ ounce Bénédictine
2½ ounces La Quintinye Blanc vermouth
1 snapdragon, discarded lemon twist, for garnish

In a mixing glass, combine the bitters, absinthe, Bénédictine, and vermouth, and fill with ice. Stir rapidly for only 15 to 20 seconds, as you don't want to overstir a vermouth drink. Strain into a chilled Nick & Nora glass, then express the lemon twist and discard. Garnish the glass with a snapdragon.

FLEURDILISIER

This "equal parts" cocktail comes from the same family of unlikely-yet-successful drinks as the Last Word (page 160) and the Yellow Parrot (page 209): unusual modifiers combined with intensely herbaceous spirits. The Fleurdilisier is lifted by the floral and almond notes of Parfait Amour, an unusual (but much loved at Maison Premiere) liqueur that gives it its light pastel hue and lends the overall drink a delicious high-toned elegance.

3 dashes of Angostura orange bitters
2 dashes of orange flower water
¾ ounce lemon juice
¾ ounce Marie Brizard Parfait Amour
¾ ounce Mattei Cap Corse Quinquina Blanc vermouth
¾ ounce La Clandestine absinthe
Cornflower blossoms, lemon zest, 2 straws, for garnish

To the small half of a Boston tin shaker, add the bitters, orange flower water, lemon juice, Parfait Amour, vermouth, and absinthe. Add 1 cup of crushed ice, cover, and shake vigorously until the tin begins to get icy on the outside. Pour into a Pontarlier glass filled with crushed ice. If you don't have a Pontarlier glass, use a collins glass. Garnish with the cornflower blossoms, lemon zest, and straws, and serve on a saucer with a doily.

MAISON ABSINTHE COLADA

Easily one of the five most famous cocktails of Maison Premiere, the Maison Absinthe Colada is the lovechild of two early Maison bar talents: Natasha David and former bar manager Maxwell Britten. Conceptually, it achieves the improbable feat of morphing the tropical combination of rhum agricole and coconut into a cooling, herbal, fennel-and-mint-accented cocktail. Visually it is stunning in its elegant simplicity, served tall in a curvaceous glass on crushed ice, with several sprigs of Israeli mint.

1 teaspoon crème de menthe
½ ounce lemon juice
½ ounce Rhum J.M white rum
1 ounce Maison Coconut Syrup (page 176)
1 ounce pineapple juice
1 ounce Mansinthe absinthe
Mint bouquet, red-striped straw, for garnish

To a hurricane glass, add the crème de menthe, lemon juice, rum, coconut syrup, pineapple juice, and absinthe, and fill three-quarters of the way with ice. Swizzle with a swizzle stick for 10 to 15 seconds, then top the glass the rest of the way with ice. Garnish with a mint bouquet and insert a red-striped straw.

INVERNESS

Inverness (a Gaelic word meaning "mouth of the River Ness" and a city in the Scottish Highlands) connotes something wild, fresh, and elemental to us, and the drink is meant to reflect that. La Muse Verte is one of the most deeply herbaceous absinthes on our shelf and even boasts a mildly woodsy bitterness—so powerful, it's not often used in our cocktails. But here it provides a great base for the Inverness's progression of flavors: the first sips are strong, both in flavor and intensity. However, as the crushed ice melts, a curious thing happens: the layer of hand-whipped cassis cream that has been passively sitting on the top begins to seep into the lower half of the cocktail, rounding off all the sharp corners of flavor and adding a textured layer of peppery black currant.

3 dashes of Angostura bitters
¼ ounce blueberry jam
¾ ounce lemon juice
¾ ounce Lemon Cordial (page 177)
½ ounce Mattei Cap Corse Quinquina Blanc vermouth
½ ounce Drambuie
¾ ounce La Muse Verte absinthe
Cassis Cream (recipe follows), 1 halved blackberry,
    2 mint sprigs, 1 juniper sprig, bamboo straw,
    cinnamon stick grated on a Microplane

To a tall pilsner glass, add the bitters, blueberry jam, lemon juice, lemon cordial, vermouth, Drambuie, and absinthe. Fill the glass three-quarters full with crushed ice and swizzle. Lightly mound the top with crushed ice. Finish with the cassis cream, blackberry, mint, juniper, straw, and cinnamon.

CASSIS CREAM

½ vial rose flower water
¼ ounce Demerara sugar
¾ ounce cassis
2 ounces heavy cream

In a small bowl, add the rose flower water, sugar, cassis, and heavy cream. Hand-whip until combined.

CASABLANCA

Yogurt is not often seen as a craft-cocktail ingredient, but the Casablanca makes an airtight case for it. What other ingredient could offer such a balanced foundation for the complexity of the other ingredients? Lactic, caloric, and mildly acidic, yogurt provides a perfectly clean canvas for the layers and details of chai and absinthe's herbs, spices, and botanicals. The drink is finished with a grated Sicilian pistachio to complete its ambitious aromatic profile.

½ ounce Duplais Verte absinthe
1 ounce lime juice
1 ounce Maison 7-Spice Chai Syrup (page 176)
1 ounce whole-milk yogurt
Toasted Sicilian pistachio grated on a Microplane,
    shaved lime zest, paper straw, for garnish

To the small half of a Boston tin shaker, add the absinthe, lime juice, chai syrup, and yogurt. Add 1 cup of crushed ice, cover, and shake vigorously until the tin begins to get icy on the outside. Pour into a Moscow mule mug. Top with more crushed ice, mounded into a little dome. Garnish with the pistachio, shaved lime zest, and straw.

WALCOTT EXPRESS

*The Walcott Express is a seemingly simple drink that recalls the gimlet or perhaps the south-*side. It has risen in the ranks of Maison cocktails over the years, and is currently Maison Premiere's bestselling cocktail of all time. This is a shocking statistic, for the base spirit is Sapin, a little-known pine-bud liqueur from Pontarlier, France—hardly an easy sell to most guests! It is most likely that those who order it were in fact admonished by their friends to do so without question upon their next trip to our bar, and its popularity is certainly not hindered by its luminescent emerald hue. It is one of those confoundingly delightful examples of something that tastes precisely how it looks, and is similarly impossible to describe, much like trying to describe an orange. But if we must, it's a bracing confection of mint, lime, and anise, with pine flavor magically tying them all together.

1 teaspoon Giffard crème de menthe
–½ ounce Germain-Robin absinthe
¾ ounce lime juice
¾ ounce Lime Cordial (page 177)
1½ ounces Sapin 55 proof
Fistful of fresh mint leaves

To the small half of a Boston tin shaker, add the crème de menthe, absinthe, lime juice, lime cordial, and Sapin. Insert the mint leaves into the bottom of the large half of the shaker and top completely with ice. Join the shakers and shake vigorously for a full minute. Strain the mixture into a chilled stemmed glass containing one big ice cube and serve.

YELLOW PARROT

For nearly a decade, the Yellow Parrot has confounded drinkers at Maison Premiere by its unlikely combination of yellow Chartreuse, Vieux Pontarlier Absinthe Verte, and Apry liqueur: all in equal parts, no less! Despite the sound of that triptych, Harry Craddock saw fit to publish the original in *The Savoy Cocktail Book* in 1930. When properly diluted and well chilled, this is an immensely delicious way to enjoy a full-bodied, absinthe-forward cocktail.

    1 ounce Marie Brizard Apry apricot liqueur
    1 ounce yellow Chartreuse
    1 ounce Vieux Pontarlier Absinthe Verte
    Lemon twist, for garnish

In a mixing glass, add the apricot liqueur, yellow Chartreuse, and absinthe, and fill with cracked ice. Stir rapidly for 30 seconds, and then begin adding more cracked ice and stir for another 30 seconds. Strain the mixture into a rocks glass filled with ice. Insert a lemon twist.

MAISON SUISSESSE

Though its origin story is as foggy as its residual effects, the Suissesse was likely birthed in the venerable Brennan's Restaurant in New Orleans, and thus was an easy pluck for our canon of cocktails. Our ambition wasn't to reimagine it but to amplify and embolden it. Here, as in other drinks, absinthe's anise flavor is complemented by mint, not to mention the floral zing of rose flower water. In addition to using the best crème de menthe, we add mint "to the shake," meaning a handful of mint is put in the Boston shaker and shaken vigorously with ice, pulverizing the mint and extracting all the essential oils, which will heighten the drink's already cooling, herbal profile.

6 drops of rose flower water
1 egg white
½ ounce Maison Orgeat (page 176)
½ ounce Tempus Fugit crème de menthe
½ ounce Herbsaint 100 proof
1 ounce La Muse Verte absinthe
½ ounce heavy cream
1 bunch of fresh mint leaves, a few reserved for
   garnish

This drink is built in steps. First, in a Boston tin shaker, combine the rose flower water, egg white, orgeat, crème de menthe, Herbsaint, and absinthe, and shake for 10 seconds. Then add the cream and shake again for another 10 seconds. Now add the fistful of mint and the ice. Join and shake vigorously for 30 seconds. Strain the mixture into a white wine glass. Garnish with a sprinkle of mint finely cut into a chiffonade.

4.
THE CALL
OF THE SEA

TO INCLUDE:

*the mighty oyster; oyster-bar inspirations;
discovery of old New York's oyster obsession;
how to order, shuck, and store oysters; oyster
population restoration; when to eat them and when
not to; a catalog of oyster knives; salubriousness of
oyster eating; an investigation into oyster liquor*

Before the 20th century, when people thought of New York, they thought of oysters. This is what New York was to the world—a great oceangoing port where people ate succulent local oysters. Visitors looked forward to trying them. New Yorkers ate them constantly. They also sold them by the millions. The combination of having reputably the best oysters in the world in what had become unarguably the greatest port in the world made New York City for an entire century the world's oyster capital.

—Mark Kurlansky, *The Big Oyster,* 2006

N THE NEW YORK OF A DIFFERENT CENTURY, YOU'RE OUT FOR a stroll in the haze of an autumn evening. The dim red glow of a lantern suspended over a descending stairwell catches your eye. Under the lantern reads a faded sign: OYSTERS IN EVERY STYLE.

Pulling open the door reveals a sweaty, packed room anchored by a long counter stretching back into the smoky darkness, laden with glittering crystal glasses and decanters. On one side of the counter, crowds of jostling people try to get the attention of bartenders, who, sleeves turned up, feverishly pour beers and roll drinks. On the other side of the counter, men in dirty aprons stand behind barrels of oysters, knives in one hand, prying open shells with preternatural speed, as piles of shells grow on the floor.

All are here for the oysters, which come stewed, boiled, pickled, and served in soups and stews and chowders. Roasted and fried and made into puddings and patties and pies. They come on toast, as well as raw or roasted in the shell. A board on the wall reads, BLUE POINTS, ROCKAWAYS, JAMAICA BAYS, PRINCE BAYS, SADDLE ROCKS, FIRE ISLAND SALTS: SIX CENTS, ALL YOU CAN EAT. A stool opens at the bar, and you pounce.

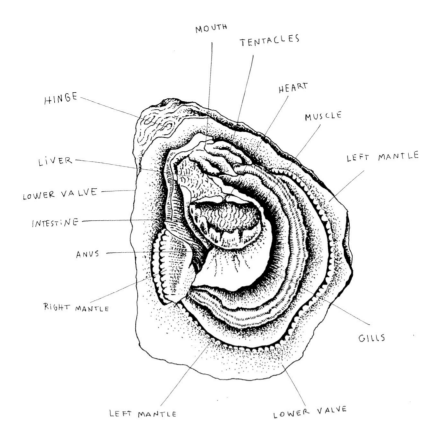

MOUTH
TENTACLES
HEART
MUSCLE
HINGE
LEFT MANTLE
LIVER
LOWER VALVE
INTESTINE
ANUS
RIGHT MANTLE
GILLS
LEFT MANTLE
LOWER VALVE

Introducing the Oyster

Oysters prove that very small beings can possess great power and consequence. That heroes come in all shapes and sizes. That they even may look like rocks, never move, and never utter a sound, yet still have an outsize impact on human history.

On the East Coast of North America alone, archaeologists have discovered giant piles of discarded oyster shells, known as *middens*, dating back almost ten thousand years. And these aren't indications of sudden oystery binges; they indicate continuous oyster shucking and slurping for thousands of years. These middens evidenced, one could say, the very first American oyster bars. Later came New York City, of course, itself one giant midden, at least for a time.

In the pages that follow, we hope to bring you inside the oyster shell and then open it up. Whatever accounts for the power of these little beings is only amplified with a little understanding. Oysters describe our world—and Maison Premiere—in a unique way. Just knowing some basic facts will help you navigate both our world and the oyster's. We'll offer some tips on ordering and eating them, both inside the home and away, and some notions of oyster etiquette. Finally, we'll give you an oyster map of North America and, later, in The Almanac chapter, a list of our head shucker's favorite varieties of oysters.

A situation familiar to most of us: You grab a seat at the oyster bar and are handed a list. In the case of Maison Premiere, the list is lengthy. As you scan the offerings, you see a roster of strange names and places—evocative, perhaps, but essentially meaningless: Blackberry Point, Rappahannock, Totten Inlet. For most of us, these words are gibberish. Isn't Totten Inlet an English soccer team?

How can you possibly order from this list when you have no idea how any of them taste, how big they are, how silky or how meaty? The intimidation is no different from what most of us feel around a wine list. But even with wine we generally have a sense of major categories: pinot noir, sauvignon blanc, etc.

If you are a bit overwhelmed by the idea of trying to grasp the nature of fifteen to twenty-five different oysters when all you want is a snack and a cold drink, join the club. But never fear, all will become clear as a shot of undiluted absinthe.

The worlds of oysters and wine have a lot in common—in each just a little knowledge can reliably get you on track. While remembering the profile of every individual oyster is not realistic, a basic understanding of the way oysters are grown and sold can help you narrow down the choices. Not only are these things easy to remember, they're also fascinating, making your oyster experience delicious for both mouth and mind.

NATURE: FIVE SPECIES GIVEN UNTO OUR WATERS

While hundreds of oyster species exist in the world, just five are grown commercially in the United States, making it quite easy to master the first pillar. Furthermore, each species is observably unique, so telling one from the other is not difficult.

THE EASTERN OYSTER • *Crassostrea virginica*—The gold standard of American mollusks, the Eastern, also known as the Atlantic oyster is, to us, the ideal oyster. One of only two species native to North America, the virginica grows up and down the East Coast and in the Gulf of Mexico. Its hard, crusty shell takes a recognizably teardrop shape, and its edges are rounded and relatively smooth. Virginicas mature into fleshy medium- to large-size oysters. As with all oysters, they grow faster and larger in warmer waters; hence Gulf oysters are big-shelled and massive, while Maines will be smaller and more taut. The flavor of the Eastern at its best epitomizes what we love: briny and mineral, brisk and bracing. Its saltiness comes from the high salinity of the Atlantic Ocean, but the Eastern is also notable for the degree to which it transparently communicates the subtleties of its growing conditions (merroir, see page 219).

THE PACIFIC OYSTER • *Crassostrea gigas*—The most cultivated oyster in the world, Pacifics have recognizably ruffled shells and generally deep cups. While it's grown from Alaska to Baja, the Pacific isn't native, but rather an import from Japan. Arriving first in Alaska sometime in the early 1900s, the Pacific grows quickly—around twice as fast as the Eastern oyster. It flourishes in many sea conditions, temperatures, and water qualities. With little effort, it can grow quite large at a rapid pace. Because of

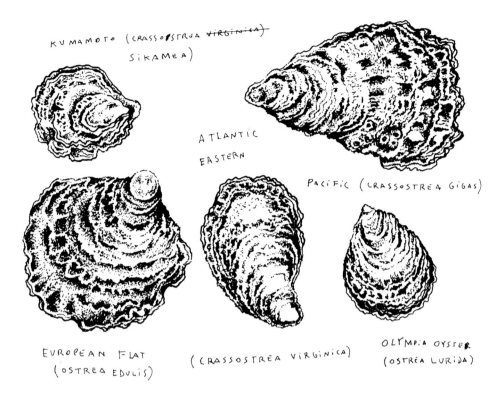

KUMAMOTO (CRASSOSTRJA ~~VIRGINICA~~
SIKAMEA)

ATLANTIC
EASTERN

PACIFIC (CRASSOSTREA GIGAS)

EUROPEAN FLAT
(OSTREA EDULIS)

(CRASSOSTREA VIRGINICA)

OLYMPIA OYSTER
(OSTREA LURIDA)

this prodigious growth, Pacifics have been embraced commercially (for instance, in France, which mostly grows Pacifics). But, as always, speed and volume can come at a cost—namely flavor. Pacific oysters have flavor, but it's not the briny, bracing oyster flavor someone raised on Atlantics might expect. Rather, it often suggests melon and cucumber and sometimes other, more exotic and earthy notes. At their best, they're complex and still deliciously oystery. But in less successful examples, these flavors can overwhelm. However, in the hands of talented oyster farmers working in favorable waters, the Pacific oyster is often delectable: fleshy and firm with complex, satisfying flavor.

THE PILLARS OF OYSTERDOM
Species and Location

Oysters taste the way they do mainly because of three basic elements: species, location, and growth method. It's that simple, sort of. Species is simple, as you'll read here. The nature and impact of specific locations are as important as in wine and just as hard to remember. But as you learn the language of oysters and develop favorites, you'll gradually start to remember more detail.

THE KUMAMOTO OYSTER • *Crassostrea sikamea*—More than the others, the Kumamoto species is a brand of its own. While a casual oyster eater might not readily know that Wellfleets are Atlantics and Kusshis are Pacific, she probably will recognize the name Kumamoto. That is, most oysters are marketed not by species but by place and producer. But with Kumamotos, people tend not to care about those details. Why? Because of all oysters anywhere, Kumamotos are distinct. They're crowd-pleasers to boot. People, especially beginning oyster consumers, love their compact size—for the squeamish, they're an easy mouthful. Round and firm, dense and chewy, Kumamotos will appeal to those with texture issues. And they are sweet with a delicate cucumber flavor, while lacking aggressive notes of seawater, seaweed, fish, or metal.

Kumamotos, as their name suggests, hail from Japan and were introduced in 1947 in Washington State. Their growth is slow, which intensifies both their flavor and their price. Primary cultivation zones in the United States include Baja California, Humboldt Bay in Northern California, and Puget Sound in Washington. Given their slow growth rate, not a lot of people raise Kumamotos, which is yet another reason why they're so special.

THE EUROPEAN FLAT OYSTER • *Ostrea edulis*—You'll often hear European flats referred to as Belons, though that moniker is technically incorrect. *Belon* is the name of the river and its coast region in Brittany, France, that produces the iconic version of this oyster, though it's been grown all over Europe for a long time. This species is cultivated in many other places now as well, though. Nevertheless, people tend to use the name Belon generically. These oysters are recognizable by their shape, which is wide, flat, and round. They can reach a harvestable size in two years, and by their fourth year can hit up to four inches in diameter. They are an acquired taste. Some people love the austere, metallic, iodine flavor, while others find it offputtingly aggressive (it's been described as tasting of a copper penny). They are also a mouthful. We love 'em.

Belons are highly prized and often expensive oysters for a few reasons. First, they're rare; like a finicky pet, they demand a lot of their growers—they don't like to be out of the water long, and they need stable, moderate temperatures to remain alive during transport. They also hold very little water, which is why their large shells are usually bound shut with a rubber band during shipment, and which requires pricey special handling and hand processing.

THE OLYMPIA OYSTER • *Ostrea lurida, Ostrea conchaphila*—A diminutive but well-loved oyster, the Olympia is the only indigenous West Coast oyster, boasting a rich history from California to British Columbia. Overharvesting in the nineteenth century combined with pollution in the twentieth nearly knocked them out of existence. But thanks to environmental restoration of the Puget Sound in Washington, they survived, and today a small but dedicated coterie of farmers still grow them. *Dedicated* is the key word, as the Olympia reaches only about the size of a quarter, so small as to be hardly worth the effort. However, devotees love the flavor, which belies the oyster's tiny size. With a sharp mineral, metallic edge, Olympia's flavor reminds one of a demure Belon. Bite-size and potent, Olympias appeal to passionate oyster purists like Krystof. Just don't expect to fill up on them: you'll have to shuck two thousand to fill a gallon.

With a stubby, rust-covered oyster knife, he popped the thing open and handed it to me, everyone watching now, my little brother shrinking away from this glistening, vaguely sexual-looking object, still dripping and nearly alive. I took it in my hand, tilted the shell back into my mouth as instructed by the by now beaming Monsieur Saint-Jour, and with one bite and a slurp, wolfed it down. It tasted of seawater . . . of brine and flesh . . . and somehow . . . of the future. Everything was different now. Everything. I'd not only survived—I'd enjoyed. This, I knew, was the magic I had until now been only dimly and spitefully aware of. . . . The genie was out of the bottle. . . . Food had power.

—Anthony Bourdain (on his first oyster at age ten),
Kitchen Confidential, 2000

LOCATION: MERROIR, ORIGIN, AND IDENTITY

Nobody comes from nowhere, right? We all carry a big piece of where we grew up with us. None more so than the oyster. In seafood parlance this notion is called *merroir*, a riff on the untranslatable French wine word *terroir*. *Terroir* is the impact of all vineyard conditions—macro and micro—that influence the final character of the wine: soil, sun exposure, climate, water source, farming method, and the list goes on. Wine lovers believe every terroir is unique and that a well-made wine can express the distinctive stamp of its terroir through its flavor, aroma, texture, etc.

The word *merroir*, playing on the French word for sea (*mer*), applies this to ocean products, with oysters being the most expressive and complex. To the eye, differences between oceanic sites are difficult to glean. Yet, underwater, each bit of coastal territory contains myriad microenvironments affected by all kinds of different dynamics. Water flow, temperature, tidal force, salinity, sunlight penetration, and mineral concentration—all of these things will affect the way an oyster grows. Oysters near the mouth of a river delta will taste different from those slightly removed from the river mouth. Oysters protected inside a bay will be different than those grown in open sea.

Merroir may actually be more impactful than terroir. In wine, the imprint of terroir is often faint at best, easily obfuscated by human intervention such as acidification, oak aging, alcohol removal, and so on. With oysters, unless you douse them with mignonette or cocktail sauce, what you taste is what you get.

NURTURE: THE MIGHTY OYSTER'S JOURNEY

One last aspect of our experience of an oyster stands apart from species and location: farming. As with wine, the details of farming rarely appear on the menu, but they are significant enough to be worth thinking about.

While wild oysters exist, almost everything we eat today is farmed. Not only have wild-oyster populations been decimated, but to run a business that supplies hungry markets, it's necessary to have an efficiently replenishable supply, which is what oyster farming provides.

SEED TO SHINING SEED • Most every oyster farmer starts with buying seed oysters. This is because, though an oyster releases millions of little oyster seeds into the wild every summer, the chance of any of them surviving and finding a home and growing to a decent size is very small (only one in a million ever makes it that far). So some companies have taken on that role. They have large tanks of plankton-rich water in which their best oyster specimens release their seed in a contained environment with a much greater rate of success. The tanks have been laden with crushed oyster shells, which is what the little baby oysters need to latch on to to start building their own home.

Seed is purchased depending on position in its growth cycle. The tiniest (and most vulnerable) larvae may cost just five hundred dollars per million. For larger specimens, price goes up accordingly, say sixty dollars for a thousand one-millimeter seeds or even fifty dollars for a thousand sixteen-millimeter babies. You can also order various strains to suit your specific location, disease-resistant oysters, and so on.

When oyster farmers take possession of the seeds, they'll place them in a nursery of sorts, where the infants will bask in temperate waters and eat an algae-rich diet over the summer, before they're big enough to be removed and taken out to their eventual permanent location.

AN OYSTER GARDEN IN THE SEA • At this point oyster farmers choose how they want to grow their oysters, a decision based on the particulars of their farm's environment (deeper waters versus shallow, muddy seafloor versus sandy or rocky, energy of tides, prevalence of predators, etc.) and their own tastes and resources.

They may choose to farm on the sea bottom, which is exactly what it sounds like—simply spread the oysters on the underwater real estate and give them a few years to mature, then dredge them up. Of course, they need the right kind of sea bottom; if it's too muddy, the oysters might sink in and suffocate. As you might expect, this method is both pure and cheap. In addition, the oysters have to fight it out down there and in turn develop desirably hard, thick shells and lots of character. The downsides are loss—there will be predators like starfish, and you'll lose some of your crop—and difficulty of harvesting, as you'll have to haul up a lot of scattered oysters and sort through them to select the right ones.

The other main option is called off-bottom, and it's exactly what it sounds like. Many versions of off-bottom oyster farming exist, but the gist is that the oysters spend their lives in bags or cages or attached to vertical lines, allowing the oysters to feed luxuriously without fear of much predation or getting sullied in the muck. Rather, they grow uniformly. Harvest is easy, as the oyster farmer knows exactly how old the oysters in each cage or bag are and when they'll be ready to harvest. Techniques have even been developed to leverage tidal action to "tumble" the oysters, turning them over a couple of times a day, which promotes growth of hard shells and deep cups. The major downside of this otherwise foolproof method is the expense and maintenance of equipment.

NAME THAT OYSTER

Some believe that names contain destiny. This is definitely true for people named Destiny, but if it weren't true for almost everything, naming and branding agencies wouldn't exist. The same is true for oysters.

Oyster brands are simply a way for a farmer to differentiate her product from the others. They are generally named in two ways—after their home waters or with some sort of fabricated trade name.

If named for home waters, most producers find a name specific to their exact spot. Hence, you don't find a particular oyster called Hood Canal, which is a wonderful oyster-growing environment in Washington's Olympic Peninsula. Rather, you'll find a host of proprietary oysters named for their particular place in the Hood Canal zone—Hama Hama (at the mouth of the Hamma Hamma River), Thorndyke (after Thorndyke Bay), or Dabob Bay, for example. These locations become in essence their brand.

Names that are simply invented can also carry a certain luster. The well-known Beausoleil oyster is not named for a specific place on the northern coast of New Brunswick, Canada, where it's grown, but for an eighteenth-century historic figure of local significance. Other trade names include Diamond Jims (New York) and Rocky Nooks (Massachusetts).

Is an oyster's name destiny? Perhaps. But, more than that, it's a handy way of remembering your favorite oysters. The next time you slurp something truly delicious, take note of the brand name and seek it out again.

OYSTERS IN LITERATURE

From the Maison bookshelf, ten of our favorite works featuring oysters and the oystering life.

THE ODYSSTER • A lost mollusk spends a decade returning home, only to find that everything there has changed.

OYSTERPUS REX • A triploid kills his shucker and marries a diploid.

OYSTERMANDIUS • Look on my shell, ye mighty, and despair.

JULIUS OYSTER • "Et tu, Beausoleil?"

OYSTER KARENINA • An oyster dares to violate the norms of the sea . . . and then goes on to pay the ultimate price.

SHUCKLEBERRY FINN • A Gulf oyster's episodic journey through the wetlands.

THE SCARLET OYSTER • Oyster Prynne is persecuted, revealing society's burning dysfunction.

OYSTER FARM • Oysters take over their farm, allegorically revealing the problems of communism.

FOR WHOM THE SHELL ROLLS • A young American goes off to war and discovers oysters.

PRIDE AND OYSTER JUICE • Young, bright women extol the follies of first dates at oyster bars.

BRITISH
COLUMBIA

(FANNY BAY,
EMERALD COVE,
EFFINGHAM)

WASHINGTON
(OLYMPIA,
LITTLE SKOOKUM)
HAMMERSLY
HAMA HAMA
TOTTEN INLET)

CALIFORNIA
HUMBOLDT
KUMAMOTO

CALIFORNIA
HOG ISLAND

CALIFORNIA
MORRO BAY

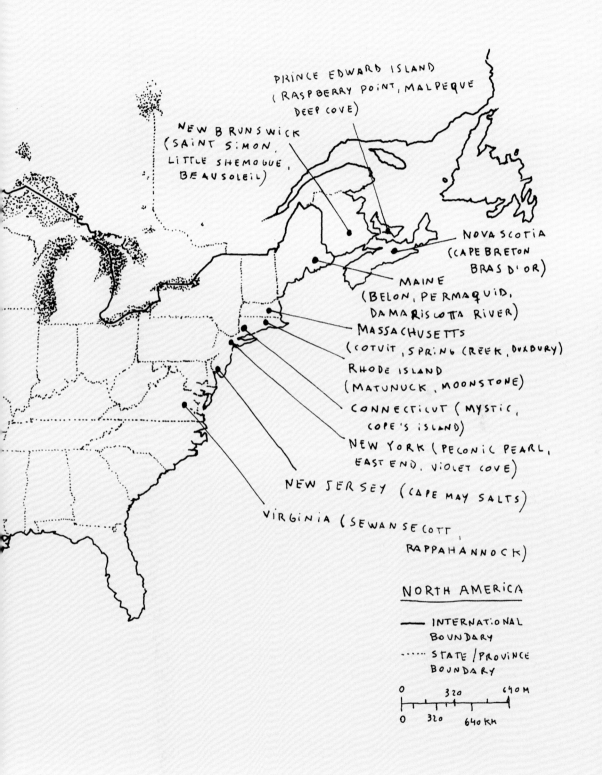

PRINCE EDWARD ISLAND
(RASPBERRY POINT, MALPEQUE
DEEP COVE)

NEW BRUNSWICK
(SAINT SIMON,
LITTLE SHEMOGUE,
BEAUSOLEIL)

NOVA SCOTIA
(CAPE BRETON
BRAS D'OR)

MAINE
(BELON, PERMAQUID,
DAMARISCOTTA RIVER)

MASSACHUSETTS
(COTUIT, SPRING CREEK, DUXBURY)

RHODE ISLAND
(MATUNUCK, MOONSTONE)

CONNECTICUT (MYSTIC,
COPE'S ISLAND)

NEW YORK (PECONIC PEARL,
EAST END, VIOLET COVE)

NEW JERSEY (CAPE MAY SALTS)

VIRGINIA (SEWANSECOTT,
RAPPAHANNOCK)

NORTH AMERICA

—— INTERNATIONAL
BOUNDARY
······ STATE/PROVINCE
BOUNDARY

0   320   640 M

0   320   640 KM

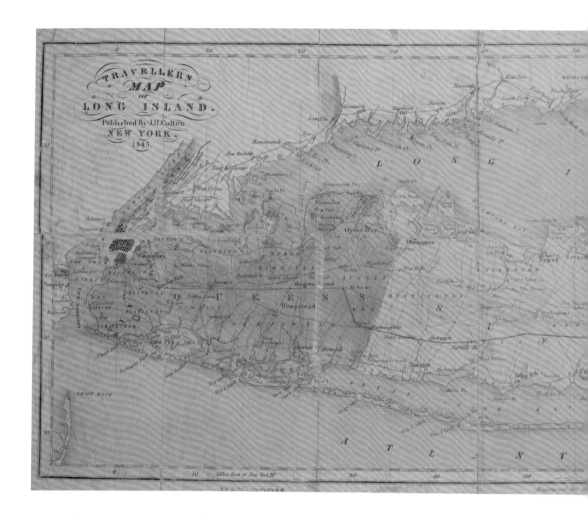

Long Island Shellfish Revival

THE MEANINGLESSNESS OF THE
BLUE POINT OYSTER

Long Island, that giant, fish-shaped spit of land pointing east into the Atlantic from New York, has a long and distinguished history with oysters, which significantly declined over the last century. But Long Island oystering has come roaring back, resulting in tons of great oysters from a burgeoning roster of great new producers. But the Blue Point oyster, once Long Island's greatest export, has nothing to do with it.

Blue Points once came from the Great South Bay—an amazingly large, shallow estuary protected from open sea by the spindly length of Fire Island and a natural oyster habitat—off the small town of Blue Point. These were evidently great oysters, and demand in New York grew so great that farmers in other parts of the bay, and then even up in Long Island Sound (north of the island), began calling their product Blue Point or even Bluepoint. The twentieth century saw the destruction of the Great South Bay oyster industry due to pollution and natural disaster, yet the Blue Point lives on as a generic oyster harvested from around New York and

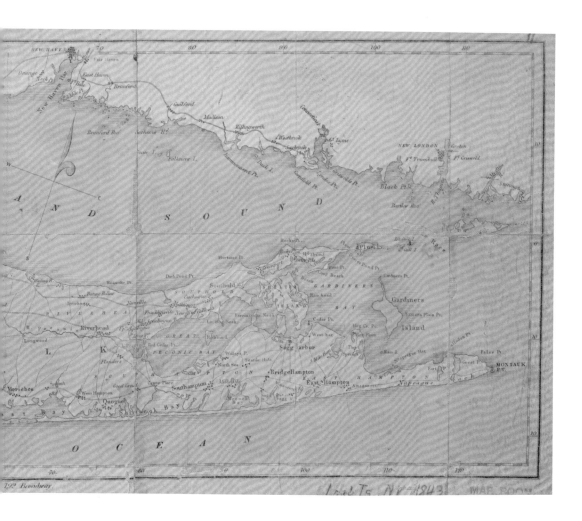

Connecticut as well as New Jersey, Delaware, and even Virginia. For the most part, they are bland, mass-produced oysters that get little of the attention and distinctiveness of a boutique oyster.

The good news is that oystering on Long Island in general is thriving. The new producers are joining the established ones to create a remarkably vibrant marketplace of original and delicious oysters with an environmental interest in keeping Long Island's ecosystems healthy and productive.

Peconic Pearls, a company spearheaded by oyster maven Karen Rivera, is a great example. A nickel from each oyster sold is invested back into research and education benefiting the health of the Peconic Estuary. The idea for **West Robins Oyster Company** was hatched only in 2015 by two ambitious young men from Vermont and Maine. They secured a lease and are farming beautifully sweet, well-formed oysters in Peconic Bay. The first commercial crop from **Southold Bay Oysters** was just in

2017. **Little Ram Oyster Company** was founded in 2018 by two women who moved to the North Fork of Long Island. And basketball hall-of-famer Susan Wicks returned to Moriches Bay, where she grew up, after a long international career. Her first harvest of her delightfully petite, deep-cupped oysters was only in 2019, marketed under the brand name **Violet Cove**.

Look to the website of the Long Island Oyster Growers Association (www.liogany.org) for more information about these and the host of other producers who are bringing Long Island oysters back with a vengeance. We look forward to supporting ever more local oyster producers at Maison.

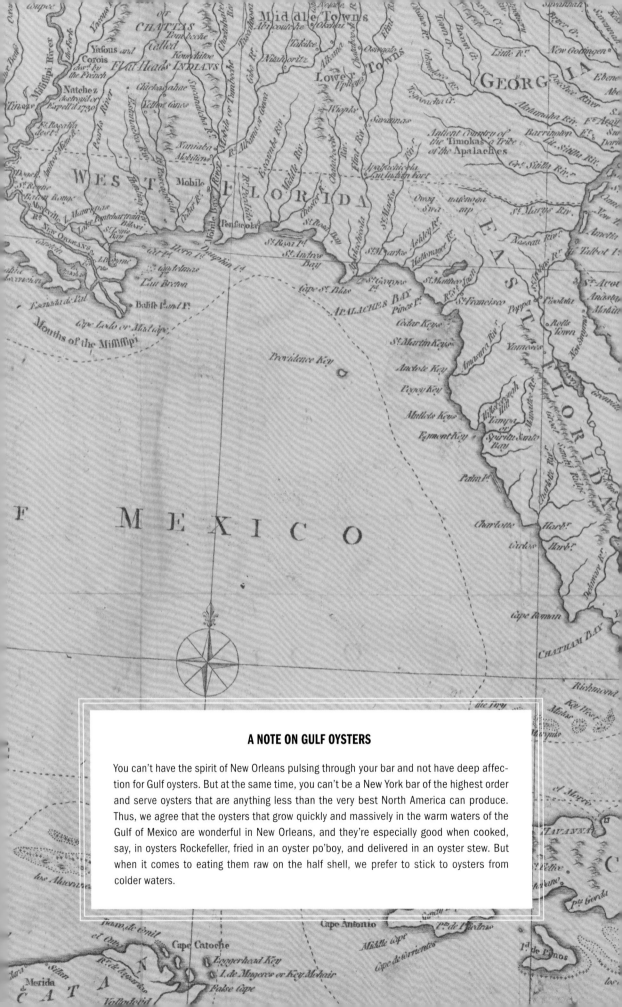

A NOTE ON GULF OYSTERS

You can't have the spirit of New Orleans pulsing through your bar and not have deep affection for Gulf oysters. But at the same time, you can't be a New York bar of the highest order and serve oysters that are anything less than the very best North America can produce. Thus, we agree that the oysters that grow quickly and massively in the warm waters of the Gulf of Mexico are wonderful in New Orleans, and they're especially good when cooked, say, in oysters Rockefeller, fried in an oyster po'boy, and delivered in an oyster stew. But when it comes to eating them raw on the half shell, we prefer to stick to oysters from colder waters.

On the Controversy of *R* Months

Everyone knows the old adage that oysters should not be eaten in months that don't contain the letter R—basically summer in the northern hemisphere. The original reason for this was because summer oysters could harbor dangerous bacteria due to warmer waters. Today, this is no longer an issue, though, as quality and safety protocols have obviated the problem. So: no *R*, no problem, right?

Not necessarily. The oyster world remains divided on the question of whether we should be wary of oysters in summer.

Today's *R*-rule advocates say there's a secondary reason to avoid oysters in summer: it's spawning season, which presents a lose-lose proposition. First, most people are repulsed by the milky texture and off-flavor of spawning oysters. Second, after spawning, the oysters are thin and almost incorporeal, having jettisoned most of their mass in preparation to rebuild throughout the *R*-rich months of autumn. They say we should just continue to avoid oysters during summer and resume when colder waters arrive in fall.

However, that can't be true, as any oyster lover can tell you that they've had wonderful oyster experiences in summer. And, indeed, the *R* rule isn't reliable. For one, oysters in different places spawn at different times, and it could be continuously throughout the season. To give up oysters for four to five months of the year would mean missing out on lots of great oysters. As a 2017 *New York Times* headline plainly put it, "Oysters, Despite What You've Heard, Are Always in Season."

While summer months can be an oyster minefield, the key is to not necessarily give up oysters but to only get them from tightly curated, completely engaged oyster programs, such as Maison Premiere's. Spawning oysters are a reality of life, but when the people serving them are in regular touch with the oyster producers, it's not too hard to work around products that are not at their peak.

Eat Oysters, Save the Planet

Besides being delicious, pleasurable, and salubrious, oysters are an environmental bellwether. Robust oyster populations go hand in hand with clean water, healthy ocean habitats, and coastal protection.

It's quite simple. A single oyster can filter up to fifty gallons of seawater a day, removing nitrogen and phosphorus—seawater pollutants, usually runoff from agriculture—while leaving cleaner water. Clearer, purer water allows other life-forms to grow—plants that now have more access to sunlight, small fish and other animals that rely on the plants for habitat, and larger animals that arrive to prey on the smaller ones. And so on.

When they proliferate, oysters themselves form formidable reefs. Navigation records from the earliest European explorers warn of navigating around them to avoid shipwreck. But these reefs also protected coastlands from storm surges, tides, and rising sea levels. Decimation of these bulwarks has caused enormous damage—most notably, experts believe the destruction in New York caused by Hurricane Sandy in 2012 would have been mitigated if ancient oyster beds had been intact to absorb the surge.

All this is to say, there are few greater examples of winning propositions for all parties than healthy oyster ecosystems. Oysters win, other plants and animals win, and people win. It's one reason why Maison is a fervent believer in and contributor to the Billion Oyster Project (see below).

Do your part. Eat oysters. Buy oysters. Cook them. Give them as gifts. Support local oyster farmers. There's nothing but upside.

WHERE DO OYSTER SHELLS GO?

*Maison takes in hundreds and hundreds of pounds of oysters every week. The oysters them-*selves spend but a short time here. In a flash they are shucked and eaten, leaving the shells, hundreds of them, to be dealt with every day. If it were thousands of years ago, we could just pile up the shells into great middens that would mark Maison's location. Today, we have another way to get rid of the shells.

Our midden, along with some sixty other local restaurants, sits on Governor's Island in New York Harbor, where shallow dunes of used oyster shells sit out in the elements. As an early founding restaurant partner, we boated out to the island early in Maison's existence for an event commemorating the Billion Oyster Project, a brilliant New York initiative to restore the health and biodiversity of the harbor through a massive community effort including education, volunteerism, and restaurant support.

From Maison Premiere and dozens of other restaurants, the project collects spent shells to the tune of eight thousand a week. Tiny baby oysters, called spat, need a solid place to gain footing before they can grow, and the calcium carbonate of old oyster shells is the material on which they naturally anchor. Without the massive oyster reefs that used to exist in the harbor, the spat are smothered in mud or swept away. Collecting shells from restaurants is the most efficient way to source the necessary material and the only way to procure the necessary volume. It also prevents these mountains of shells from going straight into the landfill.

The collected shells are left to sit for a year, exposed to the rain, sun, ice, wind, and bugs, which cleanse them of any residual bacteria. After a year or so, the shells go into a cage and are returned to the harbor, where they stack up and provide the solid base on which future generations of wild oysters will grow.

THE SEASONALITY OF
NORTH AMERICAN OYSTERS

————

AUTUMN
(September to December)

Fall is prime season for oysters. Water temperatures plummet, but sheets of harvest-impeding ice haven't developed yet in the coldest spots. Oysters put on mass, storing energy in the form of glycogen in preparation for winter when food is scarce. They become plump and firm, and the glycogen produces a sweet, rich flavor. Oysters will be at their fattest and richest in December.

WINTER
(January to March)

In winter, ocean waters are frigid (except for the Gulf) and sunlight is short, meaning there's no algae blooming, so oysters go dormant and ride it out. They live off glycogen stores, becoming thinner as winter progresses. January oysters can still be delicious, but by March they're pretty weak. This is less so on the Pacific coast, where winter waters do not get as cold.

SPRING
(April to June)

By April, ocean waters are warming and rivers are dumping nutrient-rich runoff into the estuaries. Oysters are open for business, feeding copiously posthibernation as well as opening up for the first time in months and taking in fresh saltwater. The latter softens their brininess, while the former fattens them up for summer spawning season. The result is deliciously sweet, bright, buttery oysters.

SUMMER
(June to September)

The classic danger time; summer is reproductive season. Oysters will taste great until their newly created fat is converted into sperm or eggs. This is the spawning season, and most people don't enjoy the flavor and texture of spawning oysters. After spawning, oysters are thin, wan, and depleted. They need time to build up mass again.

ACCESSING, KEEPING, CONSUMING, AND BEHAVING AROUND OUR OYSTER FRIENDS

While there's a daunting amount to learn about oysters scientifically, geographically, culturally, and historically, the good news is that enjoying them couldn't be more elementary. Whether you're buying them at a store and bringing them home to shuck or coming to Maison Premiere and letting us do the selecting, shucking, plating, and cleanup for you, oysters are about one thing: simple, direct gastronomical pleasure. If you come to us, the only thinking you have to do is to check off the oysters you desire from our daily menu. But if you want to eat them at home, find our suggestions and predilections below.

PURCHASING OYSTERS

Buying oysters to shuck at home is actually much easier than, say, selecting a perfectly ripe cantaloupe from the produce aisle. It's no more complicated than this: if the oyster's shell is closed, it's alive and okay; and if the shell is open, it's dead, so don't eat it.

In selecting individual oysters from a pile, look for the ones that are denser and weightier than the others. These have the best chance of being robust and meaty. Hollow or lighter oysters (by size) may be at a low point in their cycle, so try to avoid them. But if you're curious and buying from a fishmonger, ask them to open one for you to see and taste before buying your dozen or three. Most will be happy to oblige if you commit to purchasing.

The only other advice is that if you don't have access to a brick-and-mortar store that sells oysters, order them online. Hundreds of outlets exist, from retailers and distributors to even very small farms, and they're all happy to ship oysters to you, which are plenty hardy to survive the trip. Want to know what a wild oyster from Maine's Damariscotta River tastes like, but live in Topeka? No problem. Curious about the flavor of Olympia oysters, but you happen to be in Raleigh? You can order them. It takes a day or two, but they'll get there often in more pristine condition than if you'd bought them at a big supermarket where they'd been sitting around.

STORAGE

Oysters are indeed incredibly hardy and able to close up and survive for weeks, if not months. They used to be stored and transported by barrel. If you're keeping them for a few days or even a week at home, it's not a problem. Just remember a couple of simple principles.

Store them in the fridge. Don't freeze them with ice and don't put them in water. The fridge temperature is perfectly cold to keep them fresh and dormant. They can stay in there for weeks, if need be. Also, be sure to store them cup-side down so they hold on to their liquor. Cover them with a damp cloth to keep them from drying out, and you're good for a long time.

THE ONE ESSENTIAL: AN OYSTER KNIFE

What sort of equipment do you need to open oysters at home? Nothing besides a good oyster knife and a kitchen towel.

Of singular importance is the blade you will use to open the oyster. These days, as with most kitchen tools, options abound—from the basic and practical models to the more elaborate styles calibrated toward people who will pay for them. To be honest, successful oyster shucking depends more on technique, experience, and persistence than on a particular tool. That said, a few general rules ring true throughout all designs.

Though most oyster knives resemble paring knives, *do not* use your finely forged Wüsthof or any paring knife to open oysters. For one, the blades aren't meant for that and will likely break. Two, such blades are designed for slicing, and that's just what they'll do—but it will be your hand. Many, but not all, oyster knives sport thick, dull-ish blades that are shorter than the length of their handles. This is to supply the leverage needed to unhinge an oyster.

New Havens have the familiarly rounded, plump handles and flat, broad, stumpy blades that curve upward at the tip. Boston-style knives have longer, thinner blades. The various styles ostensibly arose to serve different ends—from shucking to serving on the half shell to high-volume shucking to fill jars, where precision is less important. To be sure, most oyster blades today are some sort of hybrid, though the most common has a New Haven style without the curved blade tip.

Maison's head shucker, Sean Campbell, prefers the basic Boston style, which provides more precision for loosening the hinge and less brute leverage than the New Haven. Both, however, are safe and durable and provide the finesse to quickly loosen the oyster from its shell without damaging it.

OYSTER KNIVES: FIVE CLASSIC STYLES

THE FRENCHMAN • French styles tend to have short, narrow, stubby blades with rather sharp, pointed tips. Handles are short and rounded, and can be thin or wide.

Deployment: Obviously works well on the native European flat oyster but can also be effective on any small-to-medium oyster. Prefers finesse to brute force. Can break on bigger, tougher oysters.

THE BOSTON • Also referred to as the Boston stabber or even Cape Cod stabber. Boston-style knives have long, somewhat thin (but not as narrow as Frenchman) blades with dull, rounded tips and oblong, pear-shaped handles.

Deployment: Versatile and comfortable. Works well with everything. Length of the blade gives great accuracy and twisting torque but requires control.

THE NEW HAVEN • Underused these days, the New Haven has a unique design. The long, pear-shaped handle and stubby, wide blade allow application of plenty of muscle. The salient feature, however, is the slight upward curve of the pointy tip, which allows for good leverage but also keeps the tip away from the oyster flesh after the hinge has been sprung. The curve also snugly fits the curvature of the top shell's underside, making for a smooth and easy separation of the muscle.

Deployment: Excellent for small- and medium-size oysters to be served pristinely on the half shell.

THE GALVESTON • Similar to a Boston in shape but with a wider and longer blade. This shucker, sometimes also referred to as a Gulf, means business. Meant for commercial shucking for meat, where the precision of half shell isn't required but speed is. It can open anything, but don't expect it to be clean or fragment-free.

Deployment: Medium-to-large Atlantic oysters (obviously including Gulf) and larger European flats.

THE PROVIDENCE • Similar to a New Haven but without the curved tip. Wider blade than the Boston, but shorter. Basic and gets the job done, but its stubby bluntness makes it easy to apply too much force.

Deployment: Good all-around shucker without the precision of the New Haven.

To Shuck an Oyster: Step-by-Step Instructions

Shucking oysters is not nearly so challenging as some would have you believe. According to Maison's main shucker, Sean Campbell, who shucks the shellfish very quickly indeed, skill and patience and feel are the keys to success, not strength. Once you get the hang of it, you'll become quicker and more confident, as the same technique can be used to open any oyster.

Sean and many professionals shuck by placing the oyster on a flat surface. Some people hold it in one hand, usually protecting that hand with a heavy-duty glove. The method described here is the flat-surface approach.

1. Rinse the oysters in clean water; wash off any sediment that may remain on the outer shells.

2. Take a standard kitchen towel and fold it over in thirds or quarters to make a multi-ply rest for the oyster.

3. Place the oyster on the towel, cup-side down, flat-side up.

4. Find the hinge: Oysters have two ends—the tapered end that culminates at the hinge, and the broad end that's the edge of the shell. Position the oyster so that the hinge points toward the hand holding the knife. Hold the oyster firmly in place.

5. Protect the hand anchoring the oyster either with one end of the folded kitchen towel or a glove. (Sean does not protect his hand with any padding, choosing to rely on his own skill as his best defense, but he has had many years of practice. He has also sliced his hand twice.)

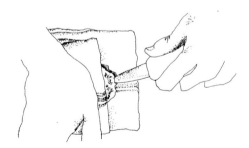

6. Insert the tip of the knife into the hinge. At first it won't go very far, but as you wiggle it around you will feel the knife begin to find some purchase in the hinge. The goal here is to get the tip far enough in to apply leverage, but not so far as to pierce the oyster when you break through. When you can feel that the knife tip is inside the hinge and while applying firm pressure, gently twist the knife back and forth like jiggling a key in a lock to unlock the hinge.

7. Once you feel and hear that satisfying pop (you'll know it when you've succeeded, as you feel the muscle give way), remove the knife tip and wipe it clean on the kitchen towel, as there's often a bit of grit inside the hinge. Then gently lift the top shell up just enough to run the knife's edge along the underside, severing the attachment of the oyster to the shell. Hold the oyster steady during this maneuver so as not to spill any of its precious liquor. Discard the top.

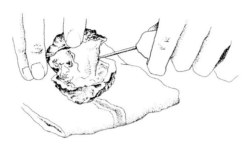

8. Now turn the broad, nonhinge side toward you and gently but firmly slip the knife blade under that side of the oyster, cutting its lower attachment to the cup. Do this decisively and accurately so as not to nick the oyster shell or stir up any substance within that will cause the liquor to become cloudy.

9. If needed, carefully clean the oyster of any shell fragments or grit that might have landed there.

10. Sniff the oyster briefly before serving as a last check that it's not bad. (This tip comes from a real experience. Josh was entertaining the famous hotelier André Balazs at Maison and a platter of oysters was brought out. They were all perfect but one, which Mr. Balazs determined after he held it up to his nose and detected an off scent. It was an embarrassing gaffe to happen in front of one of the few people Josh considers a mentor, and, since that moment, Josh mandated that every oyster be given the smell check before it goes out as a final precaution.)

How to Eat Oysters with Style

OR, THE DISREGARD OF SUCH CEREMONY

For the most part, oyster consumption in the United States is one of those rare activities free of pressure, orthodoxy, and overbearing opinion. That is, unlike wine, say, people are generally allowed to eat oysters of any kind in any way they wish, and no one gives them any trouble about it.

Every matter of taste engenders its own snobbery, and, no doubt, oyster snobs exist. What might one look like? Perhaps someone who scoffs at another for smothering a good oyster in cheap cocktail sauce. Or for not knowing the difference between Kumamotos and Shigokus. Or someone who insists you can only truly enjoy oysters with Grand Cru Chablis.

None of us feel that way. Maison's oysters are by nature democratic and, usually, North American. They don't brook elitism or pettiness. Oysters are about the most unpretentious food we can imagine; the one food that has historically been enjoyed by both the poor and the rich with equal savor. Eat your raw oysters with condiments or eat them completely unadorned; it makes no difference to us or to the oyster.

That said, we can offer a few notes on **oyster etiquette:**

THE LITTLE FORK • In many places, oysters are served with a miniature fork. Some people use it to gracefully slide the oyster into their mouths, as a hockey player might move a puck. But feel no obligation to use it. We have no problem with you slurping the whole thing right off the shell directly into your mouth, which is the only way to ingest it. Or, if you're being modest and don't feel like using your finger, perhaps use the fork to gently nudge the oyster to confirm it has been properly separated from its shell.

CONDIMENT • Raw oysters are a wonderful platform for other flavors, and a great many complementary items have been known to accompany them: fresh lemon, mignonette, raw shaved horseradish, creamy horseradish, Tabasco or another brand of bottled hot sauce, granita, wasabi, caviar, peaty single-malt scotch or mezcal (as condiment), saltines, rye bread and butter, and cocktail sauce.

All of these things can be great. Seeing them laid out next to your oysters, knowing that some cook has bothered to prepare them, can levy some feeling of duty to use them. Well, let any pressure you might feel slide away like a freshly shucked Pearl Point out of its shell. Nothing can beat the purity of a raw, unadorned oyster. Feel free to dabble in the condiments, but don't feel obligated.

ON MASTICATION • To chew or not to chew is entirely a matter of preference, though to simply swallow without bothering to taste makes eating oysters no different than taking a pill. Of course, we can imagine an aforementioned oyster snob attempting to humiliate a companion for swallowing without chewing and therefore missing out on some heightened perception. Yet, one or two quick chews before swallowing is a reasonable time to get a sense of the oyster.

THE OYSTER'S LIQUOR • *Liquor* is the term for the clear liquid surrounding a (carefully shucked) oyster. People discuss whether and how to consume the liquor. For most, it's an essential part of the experience. Whether to sip it from the shell before swallowing the oyster or taking it all together is a matter of preference; there is no proper way.

ON SLURPING • Eating raw oysters from the half shell makes it almost impossible to not slurp. The most demure of us could no doubt contrive a way. But why bother? To consume oysters with gusto is to slurp, and to slurp is to enjoy. The gesture is accepted favorably among oyster lovers, much as in Japan slurping ramen is also de rigueur.

SPENT SHELLS DOWN OR UP? • After eating an oyster, some people return the shells to the tray facing down. Other people return them as they were (minus the oyster, of course), facing upward. There is no prescription for this and therefore no judgment. It could be considered thoughtful to place the shells facing down, communicating clearly to restaurant servers when the oysters have all been consumed. Or in some restaurants oysters are served on an elevated stand placed atop the table; some diners may not be tall enough to discern which oyster has or has not been consumed. In such cases, placing them downward might be considerate. But even to have spent this many words discussing this violates some dictum of oyster culture because we are worrying too much about politeness and are not properly in the moment, savoring the loud, sloshy beauty of raw oysters. Do as you like.

MIGNONETTE

Mignonette is similar to vinaigrette but skips the oil, as it's not intended to coat or add richness. Rather, a few drops of the classic French oyster condiment adds a sharp little acidic punch to the briny, fleshy bite of a raw oyster.

    1 cup red wine vinegar
    2 teaspoons sherry vinegar
    1 teaspoon kosher salt
    ¾ teaspoon sugar
    2 teaspoons black pepper
    3 thyme sprigs
    ½ cup shallots, finely diced

Simply mix all the ingredients together at least 12 hours in advance, so the flavors can coalesce. Afterward, keep in the fridge for up to 2 weeks.

A Brief Disquisition on the
Liquor of an Oyster

————

So, this question of the oyster liquor is intriguing. Some say it's nothing but seawater, but others note—correctly, we think—that in a great oyster the liquor doesn't taste only of brine but carries a light, ethereal sweetness and delivers the umami-like satisfaction of protein, as would a delicious broth. So, what *is* oyster liquor? Seawater or not?

The answer is surprisingly elusive. In Google Books, you can find the transcription of the 1945–46 Congressional Hearings on Raw Shucked Oysters. Most of it is very long and technical. However, in two places, different oyster scientists are asked the following question: "Do you consider the natural liquor present with the oyster at the time of shucking as a part of the oyster?"

One respondent says, "I do not. . . . It is outside the oyster and would probably be about the same as the water from which the oyster was taken."

However, the other respondent, an oyster chemist (in New Orleans!) answers differently. "Yes," he says. "Since it is present within the oyster at the time of the shucking and since it is consumed when oysters are eaten directly from the half shell, I consider it to be an integral part of the shucked oyster." He notes that chemical analyses of the liquor show the presence of salt, minerals, *protein*, and up to 4.6 percent other nonmineral *food solids*. "I consider the natural juice of a shucked oyster to be just as much a part of the oyster as tomato juice is a part of the tomato!" [The exclamation point is ours.]

Hmm. This is a minor question to disagree on, yet seemingly also important. We called Neal Maloney, founder of Morro Bay Oyster Company in California (home of the delicious Pacific Golds), but also possessor of a marine biology degree from the University of Oregon. Maloney's first answer was that an oyster's liquor is merely seawater. He pointed out that an oyster filters some fifty gallons a day, "so that water is just passing through."

But then he mentioned—and this is important—that if you dump the shell liquor from a recently shucked oyster and nudge that oyster with the flat blade of your shucking knife, it will refill the shell lightly with seawater contained in its body. So, we countered, "But if that water is circulated through the oyster's body, it has to pick up some of the cells of the oyster, no?" Maloney granted us that. So, we said, "It's seawater plus!"

"Yes," he agreed. "It's seawater plus. If you have a really good palate, you could probably pull apart some different flavors at a fine level. But every oyster will taste different too." He said the liquor of a fresh oyster just pulled from the sea will be quite pure seawater. But one that's been out of the water a bit? It's different.

And therein lies the secret. If you have an oyster that you've just shucked and retained the liquor—and it's a day or two at least from the sea—try dumping the liquor and letting it refill from the juice of its own body. That is the beautiful, ethereal, umami-rich, broth-like liquor. The seawater plus. The juice of the tomato.

5.

THE
ALMANAC

TO INCLUDE:

*a collection of essential and diverting information
for Maison Premiere context and to enhance
enjoyment of this book*

CALENDARIUM

―――――

A list of notable dates and seasons of the Maison Premiere annum.

JANUARY 1 • No brunch. We tried it for a while but it simply never caught on. People don't tend to think of Maison Premiere on New Year's Day, likely because they blame us for their hangover.

LATE JANUARY • [Hunkering down to survive winter. Mix another hot toddy.]

MID-FEBRUARY, VALENTINE'S DAY • Elegant observance. We serve a preset, elevated menu. Cascades of flowers. Roses and gift bags given to guests.

MID-FEBRUARY, MARDI GRAS • No party. [You'd think we would celebrate this New Orleans bash, but we don't. Too contrived for our tastes.]

EARLY MARCH • Dreaming of spring. Begin to prepare the backyard for the garden, including cleaning, raking, and pruning; lay new gravel; repaint outdoor furniture. Scrub tiles.

MID-APRIL • Spring Pimm's Cup debuts. Hot toddy service retired.

LATE APRIL • Continuing prep for summer garden, including landscaping, flora procurement, rebuilding garden bar.

MAY, FIRST SATURDAY, KENTUCKY DERBY DAY • Kicking off our summer holiday series is the very-well-attended derby-day fête. Barbecue menu and grilled oysters. Four Roses bourbon collaborates with us to include six to eight special julep variations. Menu lists all contending horses and odds. During race, music suspended in favor of radio play-by-play (no TV). New Orleans jazz band plays outside, then comes inside.

LATE MAY, MEMORIAL DAY • Festive display of American flags from Maison's huge collection. Banners and ribbons. New Orleans jazz band returns. Special menu.

MID-JUNE • Garden in full swing. Summer Pimm's Cup debuts.

JULY 4, INDEPENDENCE DAY • Elaborate celebration featuring patriotic decorations and the USS Bomber (page 171), a shamelessly red, white, and blue cocktail.

AUGUST • Dog days of summer, city is quiet. We all just try to survive the heat and humidity. (Mix another gimlet and chill some towels.)

EARLY SEPTEMBER, LABOR DAY • Return of our American flags and jazz band. Bar features a special historic American spirit with attending cocktails, e.g., rye, rum, etc.

EARLY SEPTEMBER • Garden flora shifts to late-summer and autumnal plants—cabbages, kale, pepper plants, mums.

MID-SEPTEMBER • Fall Pimm's Cup debuts. Begin offering hot toddy service.

EARLY OCTOBER • Waning days of the garden, redecorated with pumpkins and gourds.

OCTOBER 31, HALLOWEEN • No special party, but we do acknowledge this pagan festivity. For the neighborhood kids, outside is a decorated storefront with hay bales and dry ice. For the confident, a tarot card expert offers readings.

LATE NOVEMBER, THANKSGIVING • Kitchen serves a preset menu of turkey and traditional sides. Pumpkin pie. Wines by the glass poured from large-format bottles. Typically sells out.

DECEMBER 15 • Winter Pimm's Cup debuts.

DECEMBER 25, CHRISTMAS DAY • Our kitchen is closed on Christmas Day, but we are open for oysters. Typically, very busy all day.

DECEMBER 31, NEW YEAR'S BASH • Featuring six hundred balloons, large bottles of Champagne, a burlesque dancer, Champagne toasts, and tuxedos.

ENGLISH
CHANNEL

CHAMPAGNE

LOIRE VALLEY
(CHENIN BLANC)

PARIS

REIMS

LOIRE VALLEY
(MUSCADET)

NANTES

ATLANTIC
OCEAN

CHABLIS
(CHARDONNAY)

Three Favorite Producers
in Three French Regions

MORE GREAT OYSTER WINES FROM THE MAISON CELLAR

Maison Premiere offers a highly curated list of French wine beyond perennial oyster favorite Muscadet (page 92). Maison loves to support smaller producers making wines in a soulful and ethical way, but the deciding factor is always taste, with a large consideration to the way it works with our menu. Considering that the bulk of the menu is oysters and other sea creatures, we list a panoply of wines ready and waiting to pair with a freshly shucked dozen or a tall, icy plateau de fruits de mers.

CHABLIS

The great friend of all oysters, Chablis hails from the northern edge of Burgundy, close to the southern reaches of Champagne. The famous limestone marls of the area produce Chardonnays of celebrated crispness and texture. Of course, their minerality also makes them celebrated pairings with oysters. How could they not be, since the soils Chablis grapes grow on are literally the remains of ancient shellfish beds?

DOMAINE PATTES LOUP • The personal domaine of a top young producer from a Chablis-making family. Thomas Pico has received great acclaim for intense wines of great sharpness and focus that also manage to contain an inner sweetness and fruit.

ELENI ET EDOUARD VOCORET • Young couple organically farming nearly six hectares. Not to be confused with Domaine Vocoret, a much larger producer. Transparent wines of great energy and tension.

DOMAINE GÉRARD DUPLESSIS • Young, energetic second-generation winemaker Lilian Duplessis has not only continued his family's tradition of excellence but upped the game. Farming organically in cool, damp Chablis is no easy feat, yet he manages to make crackling wines of great power and intensity that nevertheless show a stony, ethereal lift.

CHAMPAGNE

*The revolution in Champagne over the last generation has been the emergence of the grower-*producer, farmers with vineyards who used to sell their grapes to the large houses who made the famous blends. Now, many of these growers keep their fruit and turn it into their own wine, resulting in a torrent of new brands but also wines that—instead of being region-wide blends, like the famous large brands—are now expressive of vintage, village, and vineyard in a way that gives Champagne an entirely new voice. Champagne is always delicious with oysters and that is especially true of the wine from the producers below, who specialize in crisp, mineral wines.

ALEXANDRE FILAINE • The personal wine of the longtime winemaker of Bollinger, this is truly handmade Champagne crafted using premodern techniques and equipment. Only small amounts of this bone-dry, complex, and highly individualistic Champagne are available.

CHAMPAGNE PIOLLOT • An obsessive cultivator of his soils in the Aube region of southern Champagne, Roland Piollot makes wines of outstanding depth and texture. Bracingly dry and brisk, they bring the best out of an oyster.

PASCAL DOQUET • A personal favorite of one of our other favorites, the legendary producer Jacques Selosse, Pascal Doquet is a consummate farmer, believing the only path to great wine lies through the vineyards. His Champagnes, based mostly on Chardonnay, are multilayered, complex, and brimming with energy.

CHENIN BLANC (LOIRE VALLEY)

Because of this grape's rare ability to make world-class wine across every style—from sparkling to sticky sweet—it often doesn't get the props it deserves as an oyster wine. Perhaps because it tends to be rather muscular and big-boned, Chenin is not often held up as

an oyster wine. But when it's bone dry and racy with acidity, as in the wines of the producers below, it makes a worthy counterpart for even the most assertive oysters, like European flats.

MICHEL AUTRAN • In 2011, Autran decided to change careers from emergency doctor to winemaker, no easy switch! But the meticulousness required in medicine likewise serves the natural winemaker well, as making clean, sound wines with minimal intervention is challenging. With a few hectares of old-vine Chenin in Vouvray and environs, Autran makes supple and multifaceted, but dry, crisp, stony wines that are lovely for the kinds of fleshy oysters you might find from Long Island and coastal waters to the south.

DOMAINE AUX MOINES • A biodynamic vineyard run by a dynamic mother-and-daughter team, the domaine is in Savennières, a hallowed terroir for crunchy, mineral Chenin Blanc that can age for a long time. Works well with richer oysters all the way up to soups and creamy dishes.

STÉPHANE BERNAUDEAU • A sneaky favorite, this guy makes very little wine, so if you see a bottle, make sure to snag it (we do). These round, textured whites are serious mouthfuls of flavor with hints of melon rind and gooseberry, perfect for BC or Washington State oysters.

Three Sea Delicacies Commonly Featured on the Maison Premiere Menu

———

ALTERNATIVE OR SUPPLEMENTARY BUT NOT SUBORDINATE TO OYSTERS

Maison Premiere takes seafood seriously beyond oysters, as evidenced by our mighty seafood towers, buttery lobster rolls, and crisp crudo. Here are three of our favorite non-oyster seafood delicacies.

RAZOR CLAM • All hail the mighty razor clam! A delicious and curious member of the clam family, we tend to serve the Atlantic razor (*Ensis directus*), aka jackknife clam. Their ability to burrow deeply into the sand to avoid predation makes them hard to catch. The fact that they are hand harvested makes them somewhat of a delicacy. They can be steamed or sautéed, though we often serve them raw in a crudo preparation.

CAVIAR • With a history as a luxury food dating back at least to the Persians and Greeks (and probably older), the roe of the sturgeon (a prehistoric fish) has always been a luxury good. Overharvesting of wild sturgeon has made caviar incredibly precious and led to moratoriums on harvesting and importation to allow populations to recover. However, sturgeon farming, or "sustainable caviar," has increased around the world. In 2022, British scientists announced the discovery of a method to grow caviar less expensively in a lab. We shall see. While still a delicacy, caviar is also highly nutritious, especially when served at Maison Premiere with brioche and tableside vodka service. Champagne also pairs exceedingly well.

CLAMS • Beyond the spectacular razor, Maison Premiere is home to many other wonderful varieties of the noble clam, including littleneck, topneck, manila, and cherrystone. These bivalve mollusks come from sandy shores all around the world and as filterers are, like oysters, crucial elements of ocean health. Many species besides Brooklynites feed on them, including walruses, harbor seals, octopi, and numerous kinds of birds. Delicious raw, steamed, and in pasta or chowder, clams are not as complex in flavor or texture as oysters. Yet we still love them.

CROSSING BROOKLYN SHERRY

A popular poem in Williamsburg, as discovered in
the book *Sprigs of Mint* (1855)

Crowds of barmen and women attired in the usual costumes,
how curious you are to me!
Forget how we might look, madam, and throw down another sherry!

Your verse rings of a true American, went by the name of Whitman.
Stop quoting rhyme to me, we say, we're trying to get lit, man!

Finished in record time, I see. Do you desire another sip, sirs?
That we would, good lad, but without these Brooklyn hipsters.

But none of us are hipsters, sir, those did angrily proclaim.
In fact, by grace, the opposite is true and to say otherwise is lame.

A tequila then! Or gin! Or rum! Something to stoke our heat.
On yet another afternoon on crowded Bedford Street.

THE SOUND OF MAISON PREMIERE
Selections from Our Blues Soundtrack

B. B. King, *The Jungle*

Big Mama Thornton, *Stronger Than Dirt*

Bo Diddley, *Bo Diddley's a Twister*

Dr. John, *Gris-Gris*

Elmore James and John Brim, *Whose Muddy Shoes*

Fats Domino, *This Is Fats Domino!*

Gábor Szabó, *Jazz Raga*

Hound Dog Taylor and the HouseRockers, *Natural Boogie*

Howlin' Wolf, *The Howlin' Wolf Album*

Howlin' Wolf, *Moanin' in the Moonlight*

Howlin' Wolf, Muddy Waters, Bo Diddley, *The Super Super Blues Band*

Ike and Tina Turner, *Outta Season*

Junior Kimbrough, *You Better Run*

Junior Wells, *Calling All Blues*

Lightnin' Hopkins, *Last Night Blues*

Little Walter, *The Best of Little Walter*

Lowell Fulson, *Tramp*

Magic Sam, *West Side Soul*

Memphis Slim, *The Real Folk Blues*

Muddy Waters, *Electric Mud*

Muddy Waters, *Folk Singer*

Otis Rush, *Mourning in the Morning*

Screamin' Jay Hawkins, *At Home with Screamin' Jay Hawkins*

Ten Significant New Orleans Streets

In 1840, New Orleans was the nation's third most populous city and its richest. The origins of its majestic infrastructure date from this time. The city boasts colorful and historic streets and avenues too numerous to list here in total, but here are ten of our favorites.

BOURBON STREET • French Quarter, runs thirteen blocks from Canal Street to Esplanade Avenue. Named not for the vast quantities of whiskey consumed here but in honor of France and Spain's Royal House of Bourbon, originating in 1272.

CANAL STREET • Stretching 3.7 miles from Metairie Cemetery to the ferry terminal on the river, Canal Street forms the boundary between the French Quarter (Vieux Carré) and the newer, downtown American sector. The eponymous canal was never constructed.

CARONDELET STREET • One-way eastbound street running 3.3 miles from Robert Street (Uptown) to Canal Street, where it becomes Bourbon Street. Named for Spanish colonial governor Francisco Luis Héctor de Carondelet (1720s). Also, a popular cocktail at Maison Premiere.

DAUPHINE STREET • Runs 2.3 miles from Canal Street to Poland Avenue. In old France, a Dauphine is a specific person: the wife of the Dauphin, the heir to the royal throne.

DUMAINE STREET • Runs for 1.3 miles from City Park to Louis Armstrong Park. Named for a bastard son of Louis XIV.

FRENCHMEN STREET • A 1.8-mile-long street between the Mississippi River and Fillmore Street with north–south orientation. Named in honor of six French men executed by a Spanish firing squad on October 26, 1769, after leading an uprising attempting to stop the transfer of the Louisiana Territory to Spain.

NAPOLEON AVENUE • A 2.3-mile-long thoroughfare running north–south between the river and South Broad Street. Named for the former emperor of France. (Two intersecting streets, Marengo and Austerlitz, are named for two of Napoleon's battles.)

TCHOUPITOULAS STREET • Stretches almost six miles alongside the Mississippi River from Audubon Park to Canal Street. Named after an extinct Native American tribe, meaning "those who live at the river."

TOULOUSE STREET • Six-block French Quarter street named for another illegitimate son of Louis XIV.

TREME STREET • Runs only four blocks, but defines the Treme historic district, one of the oldest neighborhoods in the city and a center of African American and Creole culture, especially concerning music and brass bands. Named for Frenchman Claude Tremé, whose plantation became this district.

Inventory of Historical Artifacts, Precious and Ordinary, on Permanent Display within Maison Premiere

---

Maison is an American bar telling the story of America as if it were lived and memorialized in a bar that had continuously operated for decades. It has no particular point of view but that of the imagined slice of Americans who would have operated and patronized such a place. The assembled objects within Maison are an attempt to encapsulate that story, each chosen for its impact and meaning.

PAINTINGS, ON OPPOSITE WALLS, FACING EACH OTHER, OF A CONFEDERATE SOLDIER AND A UNION SOLDIER

*The story of New Orleans was one of occu-*pation, as in 1862 Northern forces held the city. Ultimately, the occupation early

in the war spared the city the destruction that would befall many other American cities, a blessing. Nevertheless, it was and remains a Southern city. We recognize this time period with two original works of art dating from the 1860s and 1870s. They were purchased on one of many trips to antique markets while outfitting MP.

SHIP CLOCK

*Both New Orleans and New York were sig-*nificant port towns, so we attempted to weave the maritime influence into the very fabric of the bar without being explicit. This clock, made in Brooklyn by Foster &

Sons, was originally not fitted with a ship, but we added one for decoration.

POTBELLY WOODSTOVE

We specifically sought a standard-issue antique woodstove, and found this one, basically the Ford Model T of woodstoves, mass-produced, an everyman's stove. The purchase was prompted by an image of the Old Absinthe House in New Orleans, which sported one. And the woodstove was an iconic symbol from Josh's childhood. This one came from two hours away in New Jersey, a Craigslist find.

ANTIQUE TELEPHONE

The old telephone dates to the 1920s and came from Brimfield, Massachusetts, site of the most extensive antique fair in New England. Among the many specialists there is a telephone guy. He collects solely old telephones, displays hundreds of them at his booth, and can relate the story behind every one of them. Despite their archaic forms, they've all been restored and work well. When Maison opened, this phone was connected. When somebody would call, the piercing ring proved to be grating to most of the staff, but Josh loved the sound of it, so we all learned to deal with it. Eventually, however, some inebriated customers started answering it for their own amusement. As it had become a problem, it was disconnected.

NCR CASH REGISTER

Made by the National Cash Register Company of Dayton, Ohio, this 1920s masterpiece in solid brass was the Bentley of cash registers. Its interior is machined precisely like the inside of a Rolex. It still works, and when we first opened, we used to open it all the time. Now, since it started to degenerate a bit, we leave it closed. When it was purchased at an antique fair, the seller had two identical machines and Josh bought both, in case a backup was ever needed. The twin still sits in a storage facility, waiting patiently for its time to shine.

The Top 10 Oysters of Maison Head Shucker Sean Campbell

Sean Campbell shucks a mean oyster, and he shucks it with great speed and accuracy. But he's also a quiet fellow who keeps his opinions mostly to himself. We were therefore surprised that he had a top ten, much less that the oyster to top his list was a briny beauty from New Jersey, one of the oystering world's best-kept secrets. But we treasure Sean's input and look forward to immediately slurping down a platter of pristine Cape May Salts.

1. Cape May Salt, Cape May, NJ (creamy but firm meats, salty and sweet)
2. Spring Creek, Barnstable, MA (super salty with a nice buttery finish)
3. Fishers Island, Fishers Island, NY (nice crunchy meat, full of liquor)
4. Shipwreck Select, East Point, PEI (fat meats, pleasant brine, clean finish)
5. Cotuit, Cotuit, MA (full meat, deep cup, mineral)
6. Rome Point, Narragansett Bay, RI (sea salt, chewy meat, butter and yeast)
7. Glidden Point, Damariscotta River, ME (fatty meats, salty, light mineral)
8. Marin Miyagi, Tomales Bay, CA (full of liquor, briny, cucumber)
9. Kusshi, Deep Bay, BC (creamy, firm, briny, watermelon-rind finish)
10. Glacier Point, Kachemak Bay, AK (delicate meat, clean, crisp, cucumber)

EXCERPTS FROM A CONVERSATION
with Ted Breaux, Absinthe Revivalist

In 1993, Ted Breaux was a New Orleans laboratory chemist with an intellectual curiosity about absinthe that wound up changing the world. Using his scientific skills, deep research, and persistence, Breaux ended up proving to the government (through analysis of hundred-year-old samples) that good absinthe wasn't poisonous and helped overturn the ninety-five-year-old ban. He also began distilling his own absinthe, introducing a mainstream brand, Lucid, and recreations of several important historic brands under the umbrella of Jade Liqueurs. All are distilled in the Loire Valley.

MP: We know there are many botanicals, but in good absinthe you can't really pick them out. Do you consider it a complex spirit?

TB: Very much so. When you listen to an orchestra, you hear music but often not individual instruments. And that's what good absinthe is like. Good absinthe is a symphony.

MP: Your Jade series absinthes have that complexity. How close are they truly to what absinthe would have tasted like pre-ban?

TB: They are basically as close to the originals as you can get. They're made using the original equipment, the original botanicals sourced from the original fields, and the original base spirit. The recipes were never available, so I had to do a lot of digging through archives. And, of course, spectral analysis of remaining samples of the originals confirmed or refuted the information I was finding. And years of trial and error. If one wants to know what absinthe was before the ban, this is the stuff.

MP: Your inquiry began as an intellectual pursuit. Were you an absinthe drinker?

TB: Originally, I was repulsed by the flavor of anise, and I remember being very disappointed to find out absinthe was an anise-flavored drink. Now I've learned to love it.

MP: What are your thoughts on the best way to drink it?

TB: One of the beauties of absinthe is that everyone can find the method that suits their own taste. Ironically, as repulsed as I was by the flavor of anise, now when I drink absinthe, I like it dry and strong. Historically, absinthe fountains are beautiful but weren't ubiquitous in France. Upscale establishments had a fountain, but typically if you ordered absinthe, you got a glass with a shot of liquor in it. Diluting it was never done by the barman. There would be a pitcher of ice water on the table, so you could prepare it as you wanted. The absinthe fountain offers precision. You drip it slowly so you can see what you're doing and don't accidentally overdo it, because you can't go back if you do.

In my research I remember reading some old French prose on the subject that said, "When it comes to adding water, it should never be done too quickly, which would be like rushing a good woman." (Their words.) And then the author said, "It's equally important that the water be very cold or the result would taste like"—and a French person had to translate this for me—"donkey piss."

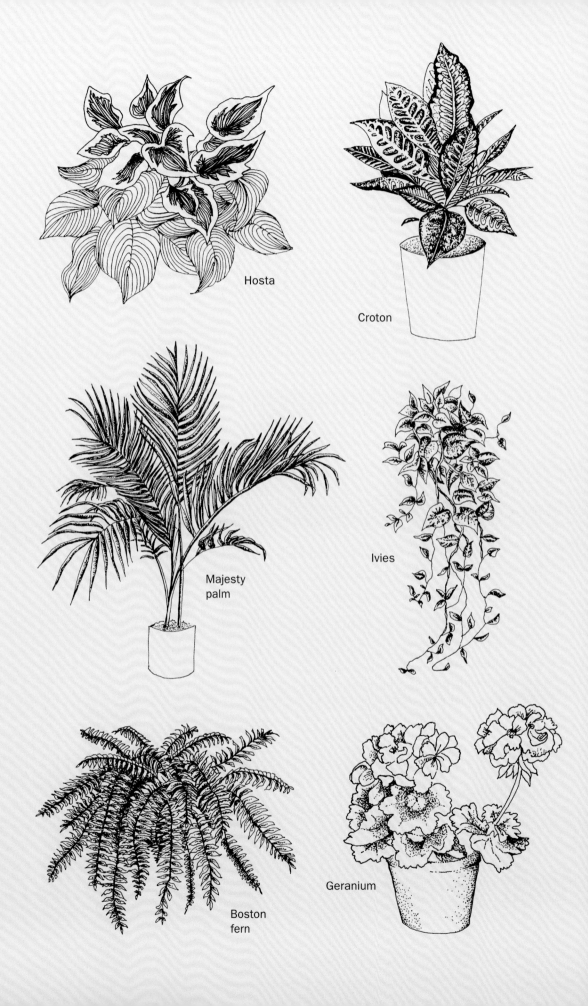

Hosta

Croton

Majesty palm

Ivies

Boston fern

Geranium

HORTUS CULTURA MAISON PREMIERICA

Plants of the Back Garden

———

Or how to transform a muddy, refuse-strewn backlot in Brooklyn into a verdant summertime facsimile of a sequestered New Orleans garden. Along with a collection of ornate, antique Victorian and French garden furniture, baroque metal trellises, and patinated garden pots and baskets, consider sourcing the following plants, each with a background worthy of the cosmopolitan port of New Orleans.

HANGING BASKETS OF SPILLING PLANTS

SPILLING IVIES • *Hedera,* genus of more than a dozen species of climbing or creeping woody plants in the family Araliaceae, native to Europe, Macaronesia, northern Africa, and Asia.

BOSTON FERNS • *Nephrolepis exaltata*, native to humid forests around the world, an air-purifying wonder!

SWEET POTATO VINES • *Ipomoea batatas*, native to the tropical regions of the Americas, an ornamental relative of the sweet potato.

RED MANDEVILLA VINE • family Apocynaceae, native of the warmer regions of the Americas, named after British diplomat and gentleman gardener Henry Mandeville (1773–1861).

TROPICAL TREES AND SHRUBS

ROBELLINI PALM • *Phoenix roebelenii* aka dwarf date palm, native to southwestern China and northern Laos and Vietnam.

UPRIGHT MAJESTY PALM • *Ravenea rivularis*, native to Madagascar and fond of a semi-humid, sunny climate, can reach up to ninety feet in height in native environments.

CAT PALM • *Chamaedorea cataractarum*, native to southern Mexico and Central America, can take eight to ten years to fully mature.

CROTON • *Codiaeum variegatum*, part of an extensive flowering-plant genus in the family Euphorbiaceae, native to Southeast Asia; a member of the same family, cascarilla, is used to flavor Campari.

MIXED PLANTINGS

HOSTA • *Asparagaceae*, native to northeast Asia; all species of hosta are edible and many are cultivated in some Asian cultures.

BLUE FESCUE • *Festuca glauca*, a species of flowering plant in the grass family that is ubiquitous throughout the world.

GERANIUM • genus *Geranium* includes 422 species of annual, biennial, and perennial plants found throughout the temperate regions of the world but mostly in the eastern part of the Mediterranean region.

MIXED COLEUS • genus *Coleus*, native to Europe, Asia, subtropics; subspecies *Coleus blumei* has mild relaxing and hallucinogenic effects when consumed; used by the Mazatecs for mind-altering effects.

ACKNOWLEDGMENTS

COLLECTIVELY, JOSHUA, KRYSTOF, AND WILL WOULD LIKE TO THANK THE great many people who made not only this book possible, but Maison Premiere itself. Lisa Carbonara and her son, Joe, may own the building that houses our establishment, but they've also been crucial supporters and friends; Maison Premiere wouldn't exist today without them. Jean-Pierre Marquet, extraordinary pastry chef and founder of Le Barricou, not only changed Josh's life with his outreach, but became a cofounder of Maison and risked a lot to get us going; for that we will always have infinite gratitude.

Also of critical importance were the amazing craftsmen who helped bring our design vision to life. The masterful painting work that gives the place its texture and depth belongs to Kevin McCormick, while his brother John created many of the incredible structures inside. Metalworker Michael Smart provided so many of the brilliant touches to brass and steel, as did Gabby Shelton for constructions like our oyster bins. The truly incredible florist Makiko Imoto brought new life and beauty every week for our first eight years with her stunning arrangements, while the talented sign painter Robert Garey helped perfect the period touch. We also thank Archie McAlister, the fabulous carpenter who built so much of the wooden infrastructure, and Luke Scarola, the antique lighting savant.

We cannot express enough gratitude to considerable talents, who, over the last twelve years, imbued Maison with spirit, creativity, and identity, including, but not exclusively, bartenders Jillian Vose, Natasha David, Maksym Pazuniak, Jesse Carr, Shae Minnillo, David Tyler, Michael Walcher, Jordan Feldman, and Andrew Shields. We have been fortunate to work with incredible chefs who elevate our menu and, consequently, our presence: Jared Stafford-Hill, Lisa Giffen, Flavio Rojas, and Beth Goodwin. A remarkable front-of-the-house staff over the years (a tough and often underappreciated role) has helped keep everything running smoothly, and we thank Cat Mallone, Hernan Martinez, Ryan Te, and all the others in that role. Of course, we thank the inimitable Maxwell Britten, with us from the beginning, who understood the vision from the outset and helped set the tone through his presence, representation, and savvy recruitment of the opening team.

We so value the talents and work ethic of Sean Campbell, our head oyster shucker, who has been with us for more than a decade and given his briny best. Likewise, Saul Tonacatl has been part of the family for almost as long, and Maison would hardly function without his effort and dedication. And we cannot hail enough the contributions of Ben Crispin, who has given so much of himself over the years as general manager and in so doing has become in many ways the public face and soul of Maison. We thank Steven Rhea for his years of service.

We wouldn't be successful without our locals and regulars who have blessedly also become friends: David and Cat Kaplan (who have spent every anniversary with us since 1898), Sean Crowley, Garro Yellin, Shyam Maskai, Ashley Knuth, Talia Baiocchi, Damian Higgins, Shane, and Darwin. Family and loved ones have also played larger roles than they think, and we salute them: Joshua's mom, Sharron, and son, Gage; Krystof's inner circle—Mila, Blanka, and Andre; and Will's love, Beth Goodwin.

Finally, a sincere shout-out to the great many vendors and producers—of oysters, seafood, produce, spirits, wines, and beer—who have honored us over the years with their products and fueled us with their devotion to the highest standards of quality. Thanks to Cian Brown for all the brilliant insights. To Casey Maher and Tim Saputo, graphic designers of the brand. And to Russell Manley, barber extraordinaire and like-minded soul, with whom we've been lucky to share a neighborhood all these years.

FOR MAKING THIS BOOK, JORDAN, JOSHUA, KRYSTOF, AND WILL EXTEND thanks to Jennifer Sit and the Clarkson Potter team for believing in this book enough to acquire it in the first place. To Kim Witherspoon, our agent, who has never wavered in support, and Jessica Mileo, too. And to the gifted ones who not only lent their talents and energy but often went to lengths to accommodate us: Susan Roxborough, our tireless and skillful editor; Ian Dingman, the book's crafty designer; Mark McCauslin and Jessica Heim, our patient production editor and production manager; Annie Atkins, the brilliant cover designer; and Paula Castro, our clever illustrator. A massive thank-you to photographer Eric Medsker, who is as agreeable and fun to work with as he is both artful and technical. We have been beyond fortunate to collaborate with such a team.

FROM JORDAN: THANKS TO KRYSTOF AND JOSH FOR SELECTING ME TO HELP bring their exquisite creation into book form; it was an honor to be invited into their small, inner circle. Equally, I'm grateful to Will Elliott, often my point of contact, and a great one at that, no matter which coast we happened to be on. Thanks to David Hale Smith, my agent, for seeing me through. To Talitha Whidbee, an amazing friend, who also eternally offered me a comfy room on my many trips to New York, much camaraderie, and plenty of wine. And, finally, to my wife, Christie, for always supporting me, even if I don't vacuum that often.

INDEX

A

Absinthe
  absinthe fountain, 29, 191,
    259
  absinthe spoon, 189-90
  alcohol by volume, 187
  American favorites, 188-89
  Bohemian method, 195
  buying, 188
  in cocktails, principles for,
    194
  distillation, 187
  drinking at home, 195-96
  euphoria from, 186-87
  frappé service, 192
  history of, 183-84
  from Jade Liqueurs, 259
  legalization of, 21-22
  louching, 187-88
  Maison Premiere drip service,
    192
  rituals and protocol, 189-91
Absinthe (cocktails)
  À La Louisiane, 99
  Casablanca, 205
  Chrysanthemum, 197
  Colada, Maison, 201
  Corpse Reviver #2, 111
  Fleurdilisier, 198
  Future Days, 142
  Inverness, 202
  Lady Lyndon, 144
  Maison Suissesse, 210
  MP Arsenic and Old Lace, 154
  Obituary, 114
  Sazerac, 112
  Tuxedo #2, 153
  Walcott Express, 206
  Whiskeytown Regatta, 148
  Yellow Parrot, 209
Adonis, 139
Agave, 70
Agua Benta Julep, 124
À La Louisiane, 99
Alaska, 153
Allspice dram
  Maison Piña Colada, 168
  Maison Sherry Cobbler, 128
Almonds. See Orgeat
Amaro
  about, 71, 76
  Barber of Seville, 136

De Surco Sling, 124
Future Days, 142
Light Green Fellow, 147
Round Robin, 143
The Shining Path, 131
Viva Alberti, 132
Angostura bitters, 71
Anisette, 76
Aperitifs, about, 71-72
Apple brandy. See Calvados
Apricot liqueur
  Missionary's Downfall, 172
  Yellow Parrot, 209
Armagnac
  about, 72
  Wharfhouse, 143
Arnaud's French 75, 100
Arsenic and Old Lace, MP, 154
Astor, John Jacob IV, 84
Avèze
  about, 72
  The Shining Path, 131

B

Barber of Seville, 136
Bar carts, 80
Bar equipment, 48-55
Baron shakers, 52
Barspoons, 54
Bar tools, 52-55
Beer. See Oyster stout
Belon (European flat) oyster,
  218
Bénédictine
  À La Louisiane, 99
  Chrysanthemum, 197
  Vieux Carré, 115
Besk
  In the Maquis, 121
  Philadelphia Jack, 156
Billion Oyster Project, 230
Bitters, 71, 72
Bloody Caesar, Maison, 119
Bloody Mary, Maison, 118
Bloody Mary Mix, Maison, 118
Blueberry jam
  Inverness, 202
  Maison Sherry Cobbler, 128
Blue Point oysters, 226-27
Bohemian method, 195
Boissy, Joshua, 14-29

Boston shaker, 48-49
Boston stabber oyster knife, 234
Boston tins, 51
Bourbon
  about, 79
  Mint Julep, 122
  Toddy tableside bar-cart
    service, 91
  Whiskeytown Regatta, 148
Brandy, 72. See also Armagnac;
  Cognac
Brandy de Jerez, 72
Breaux, Ted, 259
Britten, Maxwell, 30-33, 38

C

Cachaça
  about, 77
  Agua Benta Julep, 124
Caffè moka liqueur
  Light Green Fellow, 147
  Whiskeytown Regatta, 148
Calvados, 72-73
Campari
  MP Jungle Bird, 164
  Negroni, 157
Campbell, Sean, 233, 236, 258
Cape Cod stabber oyster knife,
  234
Carondelet, 104
Carondelet Syrup, 104
Casablanca, 205
Cassis Cream, 202
Cava
  Viva Alberti, 132
Caviar, 251-52
Chablis, about, 248-49
Chai Syrup, Maison 7-Spice,
  176-77
Champagne
  about, 249
  Arnaud's French 75, 100
Chancellor Cocktail, MP, 142
Channel knives, 55
Chartreuse
  about, 73
  Alaska, 153
  Last Word, 160
  In the Maquis, 121
  Vanderbilt Holiday, 125
  Yellow Parrot, 209

Chenin Blanc (Loire Valley),
    about, 249-51
Chez Janou (Paris), 22
Chrysanthemum, 197
Cinzano
    Vieux Carré, 115
Citrus
    cordials, about, 73
    Lemon Cordial, 177
    Lime Cordial, 177
    twist, expressing over the
        stream, 67
Clams, 251, 252
Cobbler shaker, 50-51, 52
Cocktail renaissance, 15, 36
Cocktails
    absinthe-based, originals and
        classics, 197-210
    bar setup, 47-55
    bracing and urbane, 151-60
    drawing room drinks, 139-48
    garden (summery), 117-36
    inspired by New Orleans,
        99-115
    Maison Premiere techniques,
        58-67
    notes on mixing, 96
    prepared tableside, 80
    tropical, 162-74
Coconut
    Maison Absinthe Colada,
        201
    Maison Piña Colada, 168
    Syrup, Maison, 176
    Toasted, Syrup, Maison, 176
    USS Bomber, 171
Cognac
    about, 72
    Arnaud's French 75, 100
    Light Green Fellow, 147
    Toddy tableside bar-cart
        service, 91
    Vieux Carré, 115
    Viva Alberti, 132
Condiments
    Mignonette, 241
    serving with oysters, 238
Cordials
    about, 73
    Lemon, 177
    Lime, 177
Cream
    Cassis, 202
    Light Green Fellow, 147
    Ramos Gin Fizz, 108
    Rose, 144
Crème de cacao
    Whiskeytown Regatta, 148

Crème de cassis
    Rosetti, 127
Crème de fraise
    De Surco Sling, 124
    Golden Cup, 135
Crème de menthe
    Maison Absinthe Colada,
        201
    Maison Suissesse, 210
    Missionary's Downfall, 172
    Walcott Express, 206
Crème de violette
    MP Arsenic and Old Lace,
        154
Crispin, Ben, 36, 37, 38
"Crossing Brooklyn Sherry"
    (poem), 252
Cucumber
    Pimm's Cup, 117
Curaçao
    High Chicago, 159
    MP Mai Tai, 167
    USS Bomber, 171

D

Daiquiri, 163
Dark 'n' Stormy, 174
David, Natasha, 30
DE, meaning of, 46
Demerara Simple Syrup, 175
De Surco Sling, 124
The Discipline of D.E., 46
Double jiggering, 59
Drambuie
    Inverness, 202
    Whiskeytown Regatta, 148

E

Eastern (Atlantic) oyster, 216
Eau-de-vie
    about, 73
    High Chicago, 159
    Lady Lyndon, 144
    Vanderbilt Holiday, 125
Egg whites
    Maison Suissesse, 210
    Ramos Gin Fizz, 108
    Vanderbilt Holiday, 125
Elixirs (herbal liqueurs), 73-76
Elliott, William, 33, 38, 65, 70
Equipment, bartending, 48-55
European flat (Belon) oyster,
    218
Expressing a twist over the
    stream, 67
Extracts, 71

F

Fine strainers, 54
Fine straining, 65
Fleurdilisier, 198
Frenchman oyster knife, 234
French shaker, 49-50
Future Days, 142

G

Galveston oyster knife, 234
Genepy
    about, 73
    In the Maquis, 121
    Round Robin, 143
Gentian, 72. See also Avèze;
    Salers; Suze
    about, 72
    Syrup, 176
Gibson, 152
Giffard Menthe-Pastille
    Light Green Fellow, 147
Giffen, Lisa, 36
Gimlet, 157
Gin
    about, 76
    Alaska, 153
    Carondelet, 104
    Corpse Reviver #2, 111
    Future Days, 142
    Gibson, 152
    Gimlet, 157
    Golden Cup, 135
    House of Windsor, 125
    Last Word, 160
    London Dry style, 76
    In the Maquis, 121
    The Martini, 151-52
    MP Arsenic and Old Lace, 154
    Negroni, 157
    Obituary, 114
    Old King Cole Martini, 87
    Pimm's Cup, 117
    Ramos Gin Fizz, 108
    Rosetti, 127
    Tom Collins, 156
    Tuxedo #2, 153
    USS Bomber, 171
Ginger
    Dark 'n' Stormy, 174
    Maison 7-Spice Chai Syrup,
        176-77
    New Orleans Buck, 115
    Syrup, 175
Golden Cup, 135
Grappa
    Light Green Fellow, 147
Graters, 55

Grenadine
    Maison, 177
    Round Robin, 143

H
Hannah, Chris, 99
Hard shake, 60, 61–62
Hawthorne strainer, 54
Herbal liqueurs, 73–76
Herbsaint
    Maison Suissesse, 210
High Chicago, 159
Hoffmans, 54
Honey
    Carondelet Syrup, 104
    Syrup, 177
Hot toddy tableside bar-cart
    service, 91
House of Windsor, 125
House palate, note on, 69–70
Hurricane, 107
Hurricane, Improved, 114

I
Ice
    adding, while stirring, 64
    knives, 55
    tapper, 55
Improved Hurricane, 114
In the Maquis, 121
Inverness, 202

J
Jade Liqueurs, 259
Japanese hard shake, 60
Japanese-style jigger, 52
Japanese whiskey, 79
Jiggering, 59
Jiggers, 52
Juleps
    Agua Benta, 124
    Barber of Seville, 136
    Golden Cup, 135
    Mint, 122
    Rosetti, 127
Julep strainer, 54
Jungle Bird, MP, 164

K
Knickerbocker Hotel, 84
Knives
    channel, 55
    ice, 55
    oyster, 233–34

Koriko tins, 51
Kumamoto oyster, 218
Kümmel
    about, 73–76
    High Chicago, 159

L
Last Word, 160
Le Barricou, 14, 15–16, 22
Lemon Cordial, 177
Lewis bag and mallet, 55
Light Green Fellow, 147
Lime Cordial, 177
Liqueurs, types of, 76–77
Little Ram Oyster Company, 227
Long Island oystering, 226–27
Louching, 187–88

M
Maison hard shake, 61–62
Maison Pernod Fils, 25
Maison Premiere
    absinthe fountain, 29
    absinthe theme, 21, 23
    art and artifacts, 29
    awards and recognition, 36
    back garden courtyard, 32
    back garden plants, 261–62
    bar setup, 47–55
    beer served at, 95
    building the team at, 30–33
    cocktail techniques, 58–67
    design principles, 35
    historical artifacts, 256–57
    interior, 22–25
    lease signed for, 17
    meaning behind name, 25
    music playlist, 253
    New Orleans inspiration,
        18–21
    New York Times review, 36
    non-oyster sea delicacies,
        251–52
    notable dates and seasons,
        247
    opening day, 36
    oyster bar, 21, 33
    Parisian vision for, 17
    storefront, 22–25
    vintage clothing style, 38–39
    wine served at, 92, 248–51
Mai Tai, MP, 167
Maloney, Neal, 242
Maraschino liqueur
    Last Word, 160
    Tuxedo #2, 153

Marquet, Jean-Pierre, 14, 16–17
Martini
    The Martini, 151–52
    Old King Cole, 87
    tableside bar-cart service, 84
Mastiha
    High Chicago, 159
Mauro Vergano Americano
    Lady Lyndon, 144
Merroir, about, 219
Mezcal
    about, 70
    Future Days, 142
Michelberger Mountain herbal
    liqueur
    Wharfhouse, 143
Microplanes, 55
Middens, 230
Mint
    Julep, 122
    Maison Absinthe Colada, 201
    Maison Piña Colada, 168
    Maison Sherry Cobbler, 128
    Missionary's Downfall, 172
    MP Mai Tai, 167
    New Orleans Buck, 115
    Pimm's Cup, 117
    Rosetti, 127
    Walcott Express, 206
Mise en place, 45–47
Missionary's Downfall, 172
Mixing vessels, 52
Muddlers, 55
Muscadet, about, 92–93

N
Negroni, 157
New Haven oyster knife, 234
New Orleans, LA, 18–21, 22, 32
New Orleans Buck, 115
New Orleans streets, 254

O
Obituary, 114
Off-bottom oyster farming, 221
Old Absinthe House (New
    Orleans), 22
Old Fashioned, 140
Old Hickory, 103
Old King Cole Martini, 87
Olympia oyster, 218
Orange blossom water
    Carondelet Syrup, 104
Orange flower water
    Barber of Seville, 136
    Pisco Sour, 174

Orange liqueur
  Corpse Reviver #2, 111
  types of, 76
Orgeat
  Barber of Seville, 136
  Maison, 176
  Maison Suissesse, 210
  MP Mai Tai, 167
Oyster bar at Maison Premiere
  creating the, 21
  oyster selection at, 36
  sourcing oysters for, 33
Oyster knives, 233–34
Oyster liquor, 239, 242
Oysters
  Billion Oyster Project, 230
  brand names, 222
  to chew or not to chew, 239
  condiments for, 238, 241
  controversy over R months,
    229
  Eastern (Atlantic), 216
  eating etiquette, 238–39
  environmental benefits,
    229–30
  European flat (Belon), 218
  farming methods, 219–21
  health benefits, 233
  Kumamoto, 218
  in literature, 222
  from Long Island, 226–27
  merroir, origin, and identity,
    219
  North American, seasonality
    of, 231
  Olympia, 218
  Pacific, 216–17
  purchasing, 232
  Sean Campbell's top ten,
    258
  shucking instructions, 236–37
  slurping, 239
  storing, 232
  tiny baby (spat), 230
Oyster shells, 230, 239
Oyster stout
  made for MP, 95
  Maison Bloody Mary, 118
  origins of, 95
  pairing with oysters, 95
  Whiskeytown Regatta, 148

P
Pacific oysters, 216–17
Parfait Amour
  Fleurdilisier, 198
Paris, France, 17–18, 22

Parisian shaker, 49–50
Passion Fruit
  Hurricane, 107
  Improved Hurricane, 114
  Syrup, 177
Pastis, 76
Pazuniak, Maksym, 30
Peconic Pearls, 227
Peelers, 55
Petraske, Sasha, 59
Philadelphia Jack, 156
Pimm's No. 1
  about, 76
  Golden Cup, 135
  Pimm's Cup, 117
Piña Colada, Maison, 168
Pineapple juice
  Maison Absinthe Colada, 201
  Maison Piña Colada, 168
  Maison Sherry Cobbler, 128
  Missionary's Downfall, 172
  MP Jungle Bird, 164
Pineau de Charentes
  High Chicago, 159
  House of Windsor, 125
  Lady Lyndon, 144
Pisco
  about, 77
  De Surco Sling, 124
  Sour, 174
Pomegranate juice
  Maison Grenadine, 177
Pontarlier glass, 190
Providence oyster knife, 234

Q
Quina, 71

R
Ramos Gin Fizz, 108
Raspberry(ies)
  Lady Lyndon, 144
  Syrup, 175
  Vanderbilt Holiday, 125
Razor clams, 251
Rhum agricole
  about, 77
  Daiquiri, 163
  Hurricane, 107
  Improved Hurricane, 114
  Missionary's Downfall, 172
  MP Mai Tai, 167
  Ti' Punch, 88
Rich Simple Syrup, 175
Riesling
  House of Windsor, 125

Rose flower water
  Cassis Cream, 202
  Golden Cup, 135
  Maison Suissesse, 210
  Rose Cream, 144
Rosetti, 127
Round Robin, 143
Rum
  about, 77–78
  Daiquiri, 163
  Dark 'n' Stormy, 174
  Hurricane, 107
  Improved Hurricane, 114
  Maison Absinthe Colada, 201
  Maison Piña Colada, 168
  Missionary's Downfall, 172
  MP Jungle Bird, 164
  MP Mai Tai, 167
  New Orleans Buck, 115
  Toddy tableside bar-cart
    service, 91
  USS Bomber, 171
  Wharfhouse, 143
Rye whiskey
  about, 79
  À La Louisiane, 99
  Barber of Seville, 136
  Old Fashioned, 140
  Sazerac, 112
  Toddy tableside bar-cart
    service, 91
  Vieux Carré, 115

S
Salers
  about, 70
  The Shining Path, 131
Saline Solution, 176
Sapin
  about, 72
  Philadelphia Jack, 156
  Walcott Express, 206
Sazerac
  recipe for, 112
  tableside bar-cart service, 83
Scotch
  about, 79
  MP Chancellor Cocktail, 142
Sea bottom oyster farming, 221
Seed oysters, 221
7-Spice Chai Syrup, Maison,
  176–77
Shakers, 48–52
Shaking, 59–63
Shaky Tins, 30
Shallots
  Mignonette, 241

Sherry
    Adonis, 139
    Barber of Seville, 136
    Cobbler, Maison, 128
    Wharfhouse, 143
The Shining Path, 131
Short shake, 62–63
Simple Syrup, 175
Simple Syrup, Rich, 175
Southold Bay Oysters, 227
Spanish brandy, about, 72
Spirits, list of, 70–79
Split pouring, 65, 67
Spoons, absinthe, 189–90
Stafford, Hill, Jared, 36
St-Germain
    The Shining Path, 131
Stirring, 63–64
Stout. *See* Oyster stout
Strainers, 54
Straining and pouring, 65–67
Strawberries
    De Surco Sling, 124
    Golden Cup, 135
Strega
    Viva Alberti, 132
Sugar cube, 190–91
Suissesse, Maison, 210
Suze
    about, 72
    Agua Benta Julep, 124
    High Chicago, 159
    Philadelphia Jack, 156
    USS Bomber, 171
Syrups
    Carondelet, 104
    Coconut, Maison, 176
    Demerara, 175
    Gentian, 176
    Ginger, 175
    Honey, 177
    Passion Fruit, 177
    Raspberry, 175
    Rich Simple, 175
    7-Spice Chai, Maison, 176–77
    Simple, 175
    Toasted Coconut, Maison, 176

T

Tawny port
    MP Chancellor Cocktail, 142
Teardrops, 54
Tequila, 70
Thujone, about, 186
Tinctures, 72
Tin-on-tin shake, 62

Ti' punch tableside bar-cart service, 88
Toddy tableside bar-cart service, 91
Tomato juice
    Maison Bloody Mary Mix, 118
Tom Collins, 156
Tongs, 55
Tridents, 54
Triple sec, 76
Tuxedo #2, 153
Tweezers, 55
Twist, expressing over the stream, 67

U

USS Bomber, 171

V

Vanderbilt Holiday, 125
Vermouth
    about, 78
    Adonis, 139
    À La Louisiane, 99
    Chrysanthemum, 197
    Corpse Reviver #2, 111
    Fleurdilisier, 198
    Gibson, 152
    Inverness, 202
    The Martini, 151–52
    MP Arsenic and Old Lace, 154
    MP Chancellor Cocktail, 142
    Negroni, 157
    Obituary, 114
    Old Hickory, 103
    Old King Cole Martini, 87
    Philadelphia Jack, 156
    Rosetti, 127
    Tuxedo #2, 153
    Vieux Carré, 115
Vieux Carré, 115
Vinegar
    Mignonette, 241
Violet Cove oysters, 227
Viva Alberti, 132
Vodka
    about, 78
    Lemon Cordial, 177
    Lime Cordial, 177
    Maison Bloody Mary, 118
    USS Bomber, 171
Vollrath tins, 51
Vose, Jillian, 30

W

Walcott Express
    recipe for, 206
    shaking ice and mint for, 62
Water, for absinthe ritual, 192, 259
West Robins Oyster Company, 227
Wharfhouse, 143
Whiskey
    about, 79
    À La Louisiane, 99
    Barber of Seville, 136
    Japanese, about, 79
    Mint Julep, 122
    MP Chancellor Cocktail, 142
    Old Fashioned, 140
    Sazerac, 112
    from Scotland (whisky), 79
    Toddy tableside bar-cart service, 91
    Vieux Carré, 115
    Whiskeytown Regatta, 148
Wine
    Arnaud's French 75, 100
    Chablis, about, 248–49
    Champagne, about, 249
    Chenin Blanc (Loire Valley), about, 249–51
    House of Windsor, 125
    Muscadet, about, 92–93
    Round Robin, 143
    served at Maison Premiere, 92, 248–51
    Viva Alberti, 132

Y

Yellow Parrot, 209
Yogurt
    Casablanca, 205
Yukiwa shakers, 52
Yukiwa strainers, 54

Z

Zester/channel knife, 55
Zizka, Krystof, 14–28, 33, 69–70

ISBN 978-1-9848-2569-8
Ebook ISBN 978-1-9848-2570-4

Printed in China

Library of Congress
Cataloging-in-Publication Data
Names: Boissy, Joshua; Zizka, Krystof; and
    Mackay, Jordan; with Elliott, William; authors.
Title: The Maison Premiere Almanac.
Description: New York : Clarkson Potter, [2023]
    Includes index.
Identifiers: LCCN 2022024545 (print)
    LCCN 2022024546 (ebook)
    ISBN 9781984825698 (hardcover)
    ISBN 9781984825704 (ebook)
Subjects: LCSH: Cocktails. | Maison Premiere
    (Oyster bar) | Restaurants—New York (State)—
    Brooklyn. | LCGFT: Cookbooks.
Classification: LCC TX951 .B65 2023 (print)
    LCC TX951 (ebook)
    DDC 641.87/4—dc23/eng/20220815
LC record: lccn.loc.gov/2022024545
LC ebook record: lccn.loc.gov/2022024546

Editor: Susan Roxborough
Editorial assistants: Bianca Cruz and
    Darian Keels
Cover illustrator: Annie Atkins
Photographer: Eric Medsker
Text illustrator: Paula Castro
Production editor: Mark McCauslin
Copy editors: Natalie Mansfield, Heather Rodino
Production manager: Jessica Heim
Compositor: Merri Ann Morrell
Indexer: Elizabeth T. Parson
Marketer: Chloe Aryeh
Publicist: Kristin Casemore

10 9 8 7 6 5 4 3 2 1

First Edition